The Piddle Valley Book of Country Life

Uniform with this book

The Piddle Valley Cookbook

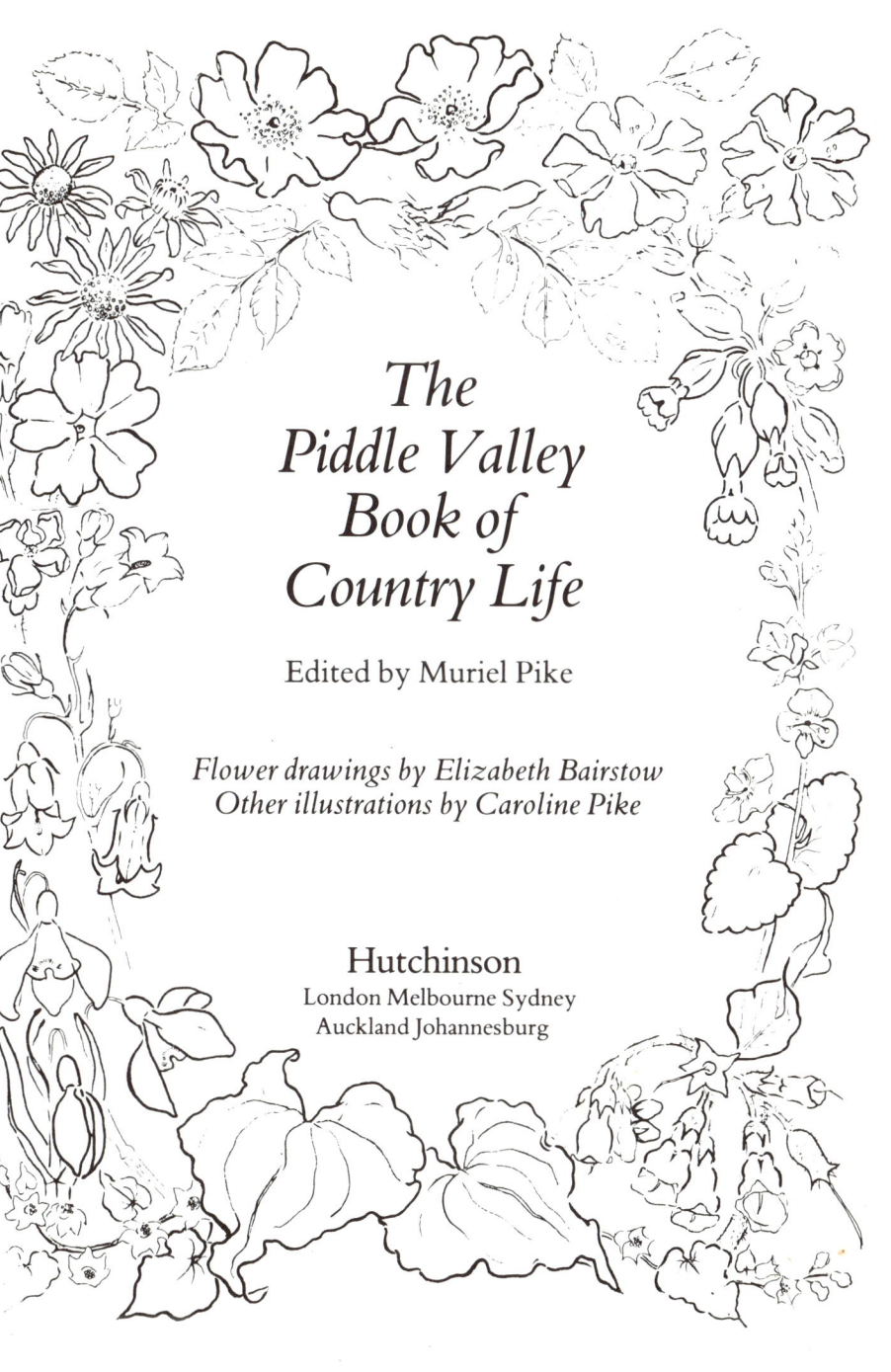

The Piddle Valley Book of Country Life

Edited by Muriel Pike

Flower drawings by Elizabeth Bairstow
Other illustrations by Caroline Pike

Hutchinson

London Melbourne Sydney
Auckland Johannesburg

Hutchinson & Co. (Publishers) Ltd

An imprint of the Hutchinson Publishing Group

3 Fitzroy Square, London W1P 6JD

Hutchinson Group (Australia) Pty Ltd
30-32 Cremorne Street, Richmond South, Victoria 3121
PO Box 151, Broadway, New South Wales 2007

Hutchinson Group (NZ) Ltd
32-34 View Road, PO Box 40-086, Glenfield, Auckland 10

Hutchinson Group (SA) Pty Ltd
PO box 337, Bergvlei 2012, South Africa

First published 1980
© Piddletrenthide Parochial Church Council 1980
Set in Linoterm Bembo by Rugcliffe Ltd, Cuckfield, Sussex
Printed in Great Britain by the Anchor Press Ltd.
and bound by Wm Brendon & Son Ltd.

British Library Cataloguing in Publication Data
The Piddle Valley book of country life.
 1. Piddletrenthide, Eng. – Social life and customs
 I. Piddletrenthide (*Parish*). *Church Council*
 942.3'31   DA690.P65/

ISBN 0 09 142520 4

Contents

Acknowledgements

The Editor's thanks are due to the following, among many others, for their help in compiling this book:
Alfred Coulthard, John Ford, Philip Green, Harry Hicks, Bill Hunt, Nat, Beryl and Biddie Kindersley, Elizabeth Larpent, Margaret Lovelace, Hilda and Ruth Matthews, Frank Moody, Andrew Pike, Francis Potter, Vic Ralph, William Rumsey, Edgar and Freda Tory, Jean Walker, Honor Waterfield and Lois Wright.

The Four Villages

The zwellen downs with chalky tracks
A-climmen up their zunny backs
Do hide green meads an' zedgy brooks,
An' clumps o' trees wi' glossy rooks.
An' hearty vo'k to laugh an' zing,
An' parish-churches in a string,
Wi' tow'rs o' merry bells to ring,
An' white roads up athirt the hills.

WILLIAM BARNES

Strung out along the banks of the River Piddle like irregular
beads on a twisted string are the villages of the Valley, with
names as evocative as lines from the Dorset poet William
Barnes himself: Piddlehinton, Piddletrenthide, Alton St
Pancras and, over the folded hills to the east, the hidden
hamlet of Plush. To the motorist, driving from Dorchester
to Sturminster Newton frequently much too fast, for the
Valley road is narrow and winding and often blocked with a
herd of cows or a slow-moving tractor, the villages may
look alike. But each has its own characteristics – its own
personality, if you like – and the people who live in them
cherish the differences.

Piddlehinton, once called by the charming name of
Honey Puddle, has a church, a school, a post office and
general store, and one public house, formerly the New Inn
and now the Thimble. Piddletrenthide has a church, a
Wesleyan Chapel, a school, a post office and general store, a
butcher's shop and three public houses: the European (so
called long before the advent of the European Economic
Community), the Poacher's and the Green Dragon, which
is by far the oldest in the Valley, being mentioned in records

of the year 1770. It used to have three others, the Sun, the Crown and the Five Bells, but they are now all private houses. Plush, reached by following a steep, narrow road opposite Piddletrenthide Manor House which winds past beech coppices and gentle hills, has a tiny church and the Brace of Pheasants. Alton St Pancras, most northerly of the Valley villages, has no shop, no school and no inn, although it does possess a church and a Georgian manor house. It is said that Piddlehinton and Piddletrenthide, until recently owned by public schools, having absentee landlords were able to please themselves in the matter of churches, chapels and public houses; whereas Alton St Pancras, belonging to a resident squire, as it still does, had to toe the squire's line.

There are other differences between the villages. When, for instance, the vicar of Piddletrenthide, Alton St Pancras and Plush visits Piddlehinton, he becomes the rector, even though he lives in the vicarage at Piddletrenthide, and the rectory at Piddlehinton is now a private house. Formerly each parish had its own parson, but today the Rev. Derek Parry has all four churches in his care.

Alton St Pancras and Piddletrenthide are separate and distinct communities. The line of demarcation between Piddletrenthide and Piddlehinton is less apparent. The residents of White Lackington, a cluster of dwellings at the south end of Piddletrenthide, tend to look upon themselves as belonging to the Piddlehinton community, even though geographically they are part of the former village. Until comparatively recent times rivalry between Piddlehinton and Piddletrenthide was rife. The youths of both villages were ready to defend their birthplace with their fists, and many a bloodied nose testified to the fierceness of the encounter.

Today, the community spirit between all four villages is strong, as was evidenced in the celebrations held to mark the Queen's Silver Jubilee in 1977. Each village took part, entering decorated floats for the procession and marching in the fancy dress parade, as well as flocking to the Piddletrenthide playing field for a barbecue and later to the Memorial Hall for dancing. Members of all the Valley organizations – the Women's Institute, the Over-Sixties' Club, the Garden

Society, the Play Group, and the Mothers' and Toddlers' Club – are drawn from all four of the villages and all meet in the Piddletrenthide Memorial Hall, built to commemorate the men from the village who lost their lives in the First World War. Piddlehinton has its own memorial cross in the centre of the village. To say, as was once suggested in a newspaper article, that villagers from one end of the Valley do not know those who live at the other end, is patently untrue. A common spirit of friendship is alive from Piddlehinton to Alton St Pancras and from Piddletrenthide to Plush, and a church fête or other rural festivity held in one village is always well patronized by people from the other three.

Some of the older villagers tend to look back with a certain nostalgia to what they think of as the happy days when 'everyone knew everyone else' and there were few people who did not work on the land or in some closely allied occupation: thatchers and hurdlemakers, blacksmiths and wheelwrights, hedgers and ditchers. There were other traditional members of the community too: the schoolmaster or mistress, all of whose pupils walked to school each day however outlying their homes; the squire, to whom the women curtseyed and the men doffed their caps; the parson who baptized, married and buried his flock; the doctor, who used to make his rounds first on horseback and later in a horse and trap; and the postman who, before the days of the ubiquitous red van, would walk the three miles over the hill to Cerne Abbas to take the mail for collection, bring back the mail for delivery and then deliver it to the houses in the Valley, all the way on foot and in all winds and weathers.

There are those who remember the carriers who used to ply between Dorchester and the Valley: Nehemiah Spicer and his wife, known as Nemmy and Granny. Later, Harry Hawker became the carrier and the first bus driver. A former villager, Harry Hicks, can vividly recall an old man named Davis, who used to drive round the lanes in his horse and cart shouting: 'Paraffin and

black pudding, benzolene and tripe, black cotton all colours!'
and no doubt did a roaring trade in these necessities of rural
life.

Today, of course, with mechanization cutting down the
labour force on the farms and many of the smaller farms
swallowed up by the two big estates which dominate the
Valley, the villagers have to look elsewhere for work, and
many of them travel to Dorchester or even further afield by
car or bus. The children no longer walk to school. The
blacksmith's forge has become the engineering shop. Sadly,
many of the old crafts are dead or dying.

In former times, still remembered by the octogenarians,
the villages were certainly more self-reliant and more self-
contained. They were inward- rather than outward-
looking. Families grew up, married their neighbours, lived
on in the same village and seldom strayed more than a few
miles beyond the Valley boundaries. It was a long-awaited
treat to travel the fourteen or so miles to the seaside at
Weymouth. Certainly it was a cosier existence, perhaps in
some ways more rewarding, because it was simpler and
closer to the earth. Today, with easily available transport
and the universal and instant communication of telephone,
radio and television, the outside world has moved steadily
nearer and is encroaching all the time, and the villages are no
longer the homogeneous, insular communities they used to
be. Many people, looking for the peace and tranquillity of
rural life, have left the noise and bustle of the cities to spend
their retirement in the Valley. Some of the old hands resent
their presence. A few of the 'foreigners' mistakenly try to
change what others believe should be changeless. But on the
whole the new and the old have integrated well and perhaps
in the end it is just such an amalgamation of past and
present, native and newcomer, that will help to preserve the
country life of the Piddle Valley.

Piddlehinton

THE VILLAGE

Most southerly of the Valley villages, Piddlehinton has
records which go back as far as the year 1068, when William
the Conqueror over-ran Dorset and bestowed part of the
conquered county on his half-brother, Robert. William had
two half-brothers, Robert of Mortain and Bishop Odo, and
in the Bayeux Tapestry they are depicted sitting beside him
as he plans the invasion of England. Robert provided
William with 200 ships for crossing the English Channel
and in return for his generosity he was rewarded with land
in the captured country, including the village of Piddlehinton. Back in Mortain fourteen years later, he built a
church dedicated to St Evreult and endowed it with his
Piddlehinton property. On his deathbed, in a fit of piety, he
willed the Dorset village to the Abbey of Mortain.

At this time the village was known as Hynepuddle,
meaning 'the marsh of the monks.' This name was later
converted to the more euphonious one of Honey Puddle,
and finally became Piddlehinton.

The Conqueror's Domesday Book records the settlement
of Little Piddle, south of Piddlehinton, with a population of
nineteen persons. It was divided into two manors: the north
manor, known as Combe Deverall, was part of Piddlehinton, the south being in the neighbouring village of Puddletown. On the east side of the river there can still be seen a
number of long closes running down the side of the valley
and bounded by low banks: these may be the crofts of
dwellings which formerly lay in the valley bottom. Two
rectangular areas which are probably the sites of houses lie

north-east of Little Piddle Farm and are bounded by low banks.

In 1417, during the Hundred Years' War between England and France, King Henry V confiscated the property of the Mortains to prevent the rents from going to his enemies. He gave it to his son, later Henry VI, the founder of Eton College, who in 1442 presented it to the foundation as part of its endowment, and for 500 years Piddlehinton remained the property of the College.

Absentee landlords, be they institutions or private persons, are not notoriously beneficent and it is evident from the records that the manor of Little Piddle gradually became deserted. By the end of the twelfth century the number of cottars had dropped to fifteen; by 1333 only seven householders remained, and exactly 200 years later only two men are listed on the Master Rolls. Similarly, the manors of North and South Louvard, now known as Higher Waterston, must have been almost completely uninhabited since there is only one house registered. Today, while Piddlehinton is still a sizable village with a growing population, the smaller valley settlements – Little Piddle, Combe Deverall, Muston, North and South Louvard, Waterston and Druce – have either disappeared entirely or been reduced to a single house or farm. Piddlehinton itself, apart from forty-two acres of glebe which became by purchase the property of the Lovelace family in 1942, remained in the possession of Eton until it was sold to Mr Ingram Spencer in 1966.

The open fields of Piddlehinton remained unenclosed until 1835. On either side of Coombe Bottom there are slight traces of strip lynchets. These are terraced strips, sometimes only a ploughshare wide, cut out of the hillside rather in the manner of vineyards in France and Italy. They show how hungry for land the farmers of the thirteenth and fourteenth centuries must have been, because they cannot have been easy to work, lying as they did along the steep and chalky slopes of the Piddle Valley. The lynchets are not easy to pick out today, as they have mostly been ploughed out, but they are visible in aerial photographs and also occur eastwards and on the north side of Little Piddle Bottom.

THE CHURCH

In the last year of the thirteenth century a church was built in the village and dedicated to the Virgin Mary. The only part that still remains is the west arch under the tower, but the first entry on the list of rectors which hangs on one of the north pillars just inside the door is dated 1295. The exact age of the present building is not known. A coffin lid dating from the early part of the fourteenth century suggests that a church may have existed at that time, but the present church is considerably later, probably belonging to the fifteenth century, although the tower may be earlier than the rest. In 1867 the building was enlarged to seat 300 people, the north aisle being rebuilt and widened six feet, and the nave and the same aisle lengthened twelve feet. The cost of this – £1050 – was partly paid for by selling lead from the roof, and the whole extension serves as a memorial to Emma Roper, wife of the rector of that time.

Only three of the stone pinnacles are still on the tower; the fourth now guards the entrance to Lantern Cottage at the church gates. The tower itself contains a fine peal of six bells, ranging in date from 1633 to 1950. A board in the south transept states: 'A peal was rung at Piddlehinton on Christmas Day Morning 1820 four hours and two minutes by Samuel Nelson, Robert Biles, William Old, Timothy Nelson, Adam Nelson.' For some time the bells have been silent except when visiting ringers have come to the church, but during the past few months new ringers have come forward to try their hands, and so in future the bells may peal out again as they have done so cheerfully in the past. It is to be hoped, however, that what befell one of the learner-ringers thirty years ago will not happen again. Mrs Walden, landlady of the New Inn – now the Thimble – was having a lesson in bell-ringing. She pulled her rope and in a flash she was drawn up with it to the top of the belfry. In terror she opened her mouth to let out a shriek and her false teeth fell with a clatter to the ground!

In January 1961, while repairs were being carried out, the removal of defective plaster revealed two hagioscopes, one on each side of the chancel arch. Hagioscopes, or 'squints' as they are more usually described, were used to enable the congregation in the side aisles to see the Elevation of the Host at a time when England was mainly a Roman Catholic country.

The church possesses a delightful brass commemorating a former rector, the Rev. Thomas Browne (1590-1617). He is depicted carrying a book and a walking stick and wearing what for all the world looks like a bowler hat, with the inscription 'parson of this place seven and twenty years.' There is also that rarity a palimpsest, a brass that has been used on both sides. It is known as the 'Goldynge Brass' in memory of Master William Goldynge, 1562, and is inscribed on the back of an earlier memorial which shows the likeness of an abbot or prior.

High up on the north wall of the chancel is a memorial, painted on wood, to the memory of the wife of Thomas Clavering, rector of Piddlehinton from 1629 to 1665. Martha Clavering died of the plague, that deadly epidemic of the seventeenth century, while she was ministering to the sick of the parish. The inscription, in Latin, is both eloquent and inexpressibly moving and a translation is surely worth quoting in its entirety:

John, first-born son of Thomas Clavering, sweet infant babe, taken away from his mother's bosom, was laid low on the 18th day of April, 1644, and with him is laid Martha, the most devoted mother of the said child and of nine children more. A wife most faithful to her husband, she was descended from the families of the Souths of Swallowcliff, in the county of Wilts, and of the Butlers of the county of Dorset. She was a cheerful housewife, a matron of spotless chastity, most prudent, calm, and gracious. In beauty of bodily form and of mind she was lovely and loveable. In pressing forward every good work she was at once most ready herself in its pursuit, and likewise instigated others to follow it. In her piety she was neither ostentatious nor superficial, but in a natural manner religious and inwardly devoted to her God. A lady of most engaging manners, combined with serious behaviour, she attached to herself all who knew her by loving and dutiful service. Whatsoever accident might befall, she manifested a quiet and unruffled spirit resigned to the will of her Heavenly Father. Worthy she was above all others to be held in perpetual remembrance and her example deserves to be followed as a pattern. The dearest, congenial and most deeply lamented spouse. While with a too ready and forward kindliness she was intent on caring diligently for the health of others, thinking alas too little of her own, she was seized by the malignant epidemic disease which she was busily engaged in tending. She cast herself resolutely upon the arms of the Saviour Jesus, and on a night which was so sad a time for us, but for herself the Dawning of the Day, on May 22nd, 1664, she fell asleep gently in the Lord in the course of her six and fortieth year. It was her husband's wish to ascribe to her memory this record of their unbroken harmony, and of her worth which cannot ever be sufficiently extolled, as a tribute which Truth and Love demand. In his bereavement he is forlorn, rendered inevitably a sorrowing mourner: like the night raven wakeful in the house, or as the sparrow left alone upon the housetop.

T. C. her husband. She has gone before. I shall follow. We shall live again.

Nay! he who wrote the preceding lines *has* now already followed to the place whither he taught her to lead the way. Mr Thomas Clavering, the excellent Rector and Ornament of this Church, dying on the 29th of October, in the year of our Lord 1665, in the 66th year of his age.

Thou knowest not at what hour: therefore watch.

About seventy-five years ago the then rector of Piddlehinton, the Rev. J.E. Hawksley, had a habit of wearing a large, full black cassock when giving the school children their scripture lessons. He would put his hands in his pockets, spread out the skirts of the cassock and stand in front of the fire so that no one else in the schoolroom could see it or feel its warmth. One of the children, Bertha Payne, in later years told her daughter, Amy Neades, that one day, 'Rector did begin to smoke and was proper put out!'

THE RESURRECTION OF THE PIDDLEHINTON 'CLORK'

A turret clock was recently discovered in Piddlehinton church tower, where it had lain neglected for many years. It is said that when Mr Tom Tribe of Sturminster Newton, an international expert on antique clocks, saw it for the first time he was so interested that he was rendered speechless for five minutes!

Research has revealed that it was made by Lawrence Boyce of Puddletown, a well-known local clock-maker who made the somewhat similar clock formerly in Bere Regis Church and now on display in the County Museum in Dorchester. Boyce, who died in 1738, and his son John (1699-1766) were skilled craftsmen, as is shown by their still-surviving long-case clocks, and they were the proprietors of a thriving business in this part of Dorset, repairing church bells and making locks as well as making and repairing both turret and domestic timepieces.

The Piddlehinton clock was apparently made in 1730 to replace an earlier clock made by Ralph Cloud of Beaminster, who was paid £5 in 1697 'for makinge ye clork.' Even this may not have been the church's first clock, for there is an entry in the churchwardens' accounts for the year 1686 which says: 'Pd Wm Arnol for the clork used in the former churchwardens times . . . 2d.' This perhaps alludes to the sale of the original clock before the arrival of the new one made by Cloud.

After the entries mentioning Ralph Cloud, subsequent entries in the churchwardens' accounts clearly relate to the present, newly-discovered clock:

1730, October	Expenses with Mr Boyes in bargaining for the clork	5	0
	For fetching the clork and expenses	6	0
	Paid at finishing of clork	6	0
	Expenses wen M. Boyes came for the money	1	0
	Paid Mr Boyes for the clork	12 12	0
	Paid Mr Boyes for the lock of the tower door	2	6
	Paid Mr Boyes for items and nails	1	6

Following his father's death in 1738, John Boyce continued to service the clock for a further eight years, making an annual visit to the church for this purpose. An entry of 1744 states: 'Paid John Boice for cleaning the clock 5s.' After 1746 Boyce seems to have given up his contract with the Piddlehinton church authorities, as his name does not appear any more. Instead, his duties were taken over by William Rogers, the village blacksmith, who was still carrying out the annual task (now for the princely sum of 7s. 6d. per annum) when the records end in 1766.

The frame of the clock is made entirely of wrought iron, possibly imported from Sweden since it is constructed wholly of bar stock of a type associated with contemporary Swedish foundries. It is of an unusual design, having the two trains of wheels set one behind the other instead of side by side as was the normal pattern by that time. It would have been driven by two weights, probably of lead but maybe of stone or iron, and regulated by a pendulum some forty-two inches long with a period of just over one second. It would have been necessary to wind it every day and this would have been accomplished by turning the capstans on the wooden barrels to raise the weights. For this daily service the clerk was paid 6s. each half year. A sundial would have been consulted periodically to make sure that the clock showed the correct time.

The clock is now on view in Piddlehinton Church.

JIM HOOPER
Headmaster, Piddletrenthide School

A HEROINE OF WATERLOO

Everyone knows of Florence Nightingale. Few people if any, have heard of Ann Winzer. Yet forty years before the Lady with the Lamp carried her symbolic light through the field hospitals of the Crimea, Ann Winzer was bringing medical help and comfort to casualties on the battlefield of Waterloo, perhaps even assisting Dr John Hume, Wellington's personal surgeon, with the operations he had to perform on the wounded without, of course, benefit of anaesthetics or modern drugs. Conditions at Waterloo were little better than the appalling conditions Miss Nightingale had to face. Torrents of rain had fallen the day before the battle and everywhere was a sea of mud. The number of casualties was enormous – 12,000 British and Hanoverians, 25,000 French and over 7000 Prussians – and stretcher parties were continually arriving at makeshift field hospitals at the rear of the line. Ann Winzer can surely never have anticipated such horrors when she accompanied the British forces overseas.

Her tombstone, close to the north boundary of Piddle-hinton churchyard, tells it all:

SACRED

TO

THE MEMORY OF

ANN

THE BELOVED WIFE OF

JAMES WINZER

WHO DEPARTED THIS LIFE

NOVEMBER 28TH 1873

AGED 82 YEARS

She was a Waterloo heroine who assisted at that famous battle AD 1815 by aiding & assisting the sick & wounded. She endured many hardships having followed the British army from Brussels to Paris. From Paris to Duney. Returned to England & from thence to the Rock of Gibraltar where she remained 4 years. She afterwards resided in this parish where she received a pension through the instrumentality of Colonel Astell with that of many other officers by whose kindness this stone is raised as a tribute of respect to a long life spent in true & faithful service.

There are those who believe that Ann Winzer accompanied Florence Nightingale to Russia and gave the benefit of her experience to that more renowned lady. But as she would almost certainly have reached the age of sixty by that time, the conjecture is more likely to be fiction than fact.

THE PIDDLEHINTON DOLE

One pound of bread, a mince pie and a pint of ale: this was the dole that used to be handed out every Christmas-tide from time immemorial to each parishioner of Piddlehinton, man, woman and child, rich and poor, householder and tenant, oldest inhabitant and most recent newcomer.

Tradition says that the mince pies were large, big enough to be cut into four, each quarter being sufficient for one person, and that the pastry and bread – designed to offset the richness of the meat – were baked in an oven built specially for the purpose in the rectory kitchen. No one has discovered how the custom originated, but it is certain that for countless years successive rectors were obliged to find out of their own resources a sum in the neighbourhood of £9 or £10 a year to pay for the dole.

There came a time, in the year 1839, when the then rector, the Rev. Thomas Carter, decided to put his foot down and make an end to it. The drain on his pocket was becoming greater every year and was in many cases benefitting parishioners far better off than himself. Accordingly he preached a sermon shortly before Christmas telling the congregation of his plan to discontinue the dole and substitute a Relief Fund for the poor and needy in its place.

The decision was not favourably received. Many parishioners, even the wealthiest who had no need of charity, looked upon the dole as their right. They demanded that it should still be forthcoming and threatened to withhold their tithes if it were not. Worst of all, in Thomas Carter's own words, they showed 'a kind of democratic independence of spirit' which could lead only to violence and even anarchy.

In face of this opposition, the Rector applied to Eton College, in whose gift the living was, for leave to give up the dole. He pointed out that nothing in the parish records established it as a prescribed right and that other and better ways could be found for assisting those in need. Not only the deserving poor, he observed, but 'persons of bad character, illegitimate children etc. were benefitted indiscriminately with the most respectable,' and tempers had been so raised in the past that a previous rector was 'violently assaulted by a small party demanding their due because the cart conveying the articles from Dorchester was delayed beyond its expected time by the snow.' He also pointed out that an increase in the population could lay an even heavier burden on the rector's resources; such an increase was likely as 'there is a great probability of a high road being made through the village.'

When the day of distribution arrived many parishioners turned up demanding their pies as a right and refusing 'in a very unbecoming manner' to be gainsaid. These Carter refused to satisfy unless, as he said, the right could be legally proved. Others, who came in a more amenable spirit, were awarded their pies and ale. For the most part, the poor seemed to prefer the idea of a Relief Fund and agreed to join it by subscribing a small amount each week which would be refunded with interest at the end of the year.

The following Christmas, Carter continued reluctantly to hand out the dole to all who came for it, excepting the ringleaders of the previous year's disturbance, 'whom I thought necessary to mark as examples'. Four of the principal farmers, in their turn, refused to pay their tithes until what they termed the 'rights of the parish' were restored.

Carter, however, was a strong-minded man. He would not be brow-beaten and the Provost and Fellows of Eton upheld his proposal, acknowledging that the parish of Piddlehinton had no valid claim on the rector for a Christmas dole. Legal opinion enforced the decision. Thomas Carter published an address to his parishioners again setting out his reasons for discontinuing the practice, and from that time the Piddlehinton Dole ceased to exist.

EIGHTEENTH-CENTURY ALMSGIVING

The accounts of the Overseers of the Parish of Piddlehinton, whose duty it was to distribute alms to the poor, paint a vivid picture of the poverty that haunted rural areas 250 years ago. The same names crop up in the ledger again and again, particularly that of a certain Honour Vincent, described variously as 'Vensen', 'Vensent' and 'Vencent':

1745

Jun	20	Paid for mending honour vensens shoes		10d.
Aug	23	paid for mending honour vencents shoes		2d.
Oct	1	paid for mending honour vensens shoes		5d.
Nov		paide for a new paire of shoes for honour vencent	2s.	6d.

1747

Mar	25	Paid for six ounces of yarn to make honour vincent storkings at 2 pence the ounce	1s.	0d.
Mar	26	paid for a hat for honour vensent	1s.	0d.
		paid for a new paire of shoes honour vensent	2s.	6d.

1748

May	25	Paid for Honor Vincents bodes (bodice)	3s.	0d.
Aug	12	Paid for an apron for Honor Vincent	1s.	6d.
Sep	29	paid for to shifts for Honour Vincent	5s.	6d.
		and for a cote for Honour Vincent	4s.	1½d.

There is also an intriguing entry for 16 March 1747, which no doubt alludes to the same family:

Paide Joseph Grose for two hourses and his daughter to carry Edward Vensents wife to pool	6s.	0d.
Paide the Churchwardens for going to pool with Edward Vensents wife	2s.	0d.
Paid for eatabls and drinkabls on the road to pool	3s.	2d.
Paid charges for their horses on the road to pool	2s.	6d.
Paid for caring [carrying] Edward Vensents wife from pool to Christ Church	4s.	0d.

No reason is given for Mistress Vincent's journey to Poole and from there to Christchurch, and no explanation as to why the churchwardens of Piddlehinton had to accompany her.

Eighteen years later the Vincent family were still a drain on the parish resources:

1765

bought Ned Vincent maid to aprons, a hat & strings, 3 pairs of hosen, a pair of shoes, Lency [linsey] at 1s. 6d. & making her Coat, 2 handkerchief, a pair of stays, a Cloke & a pair of pattens

until the following year a final payment was made:

1766

Payment for Ned Vincent in his sickness and buriall For caring Ned Vincent Daughter into blackmore to get her a place and for my hinderence and expense in bargening for her and for going up to Piddle twice to weight upon him in his Sickness and to Puddletown to by him Close [buy him clothes]   3s.   0d.

Other entries show how many different parishioners were in receipt of the Overseers' alms and for what diverse purposes:

1746

march 31	Alowed the widdow Tizard for being Sara Mosses midwife	2s. 0d.

1749

April 24	Gave Will. Channing by concent of a vestry for cleaning his family out of the smallpox	1s. 0d.
Oct ye 9	Reserved for Elizabeth Loman at farmer Paules house at Crockington in buckland hundred 1 fether bead, 1 beadstead, 1 bolester, 2 pillars, 3 blankits, 3 sheats, 1 puter Dish, Skillit, 1 warming pan, 1 pair of tongs, 1 iron pot, A baseing ladle, 1 Rug, 1 quilt for her use.	
	Sold the residue of her goods to Farmer paul as follow	
	28 pound of puter at 5d. ye pound	11s. 8d.
	A large belmettle pot 29 pound at 4d. ye pound	9s. 8d.
	40 pound of old iron	3s. 4d.
	A brass candlestick a cimer a little kittle	2s. 6d.
	4 joint stools	2s. 6d.
	ye boards of ye table	2s. 6d.
	ye settle	2s. 6d.

	A box & to old tubs and trendles	4s.	6d.
	1 pair of tonges A old skillet	2s.	0d.

1750

June ye 3rd Gave Jams Hore in his sickness   2s. 0d.
     10th pd for a Cofing for James Hore   8s. 0d.
          pd for his Shroud   2s. 8d.
          pd for Layeing him out   1s. 0d.
          pd for diging his grave   1s. 0d.
          pd for Ringing the Bell   1s. 0d.
          pd for ye Affadavit   6d.

1753

July ye 12   paid at the veshture for Dresing Betty Low-
mans legs   16s. 0d.

1762

March 2   Paid for Physick for M. Hoar (being bit by a
cat)   2s. 0d.

1766

April 27   For my going to Mapowdr to enquire where
[whether] John Day was lawfully married
or not   3s. 0d.

1777

May 4   Paid for warrant to apprehend Edward
Edmunds for a Bastard by Sarah Ozard   2s. 0d.

There is also an astonishingly large amount of goods given to a sick man, one William Randell, throughout the month of April 1768:

1 bushel of barley
1 week's tenden (tending) by Susan Moore
furze fagets
2 peck of wheate
oate meal
for horse an men going to Cerne and Dorchester for the two dockters when he was worse
1 galon of strong bear
a botel of brandy
for a neck of mutn
1 pd of candels
1 pd of shuger

And finally the two 'dockters' were paid:

Dockter Buckland £22 2s. 0d.
Dockter Meech £19 19 0d

Mrs Ellen Trevett was an old lady who used to lay out the dead and bring in the babies. One day the late Mrs Lovelace met her in Piddlehinton High Street and asked her:

'Where are you going, Mrs Trevett?'

'I've got to go up to Ambrose Brown's,' she answered. 'He've died.'

Soon afterwards, Mrs Lovelace was looking out of the window of her house and saw Mrs Trevett coming back.

'You've been quick,' she said.

'Well,' Mrs Trevett told her, 'I went up to Ambrose Brown's and turned back the sheet off his face and he said: "What be you come vor, Mrs Trevett? I 'aven't 'ad me breakfast yet!"'

Sadly, Mr Brown did in fact die a few days later.

Small Piddlehinton boy: 'Hens sit on eggs and have chickens – cats sit on taties and have kittens – what did you sit on, our Mam?'

Old Mrs Lovelace's advice to her son, Rex, and future daughter-in-law, Margaret, when they were courting:

'Always let the night's diversion withstand the morning's inspection!'

Piddlehinton man's reply to the question: 'How do you keep going during the day?'

'I have a dew bit, a stay bit, a nammit, a crummit, and then a wee bit after supper!'

(*Glossary*: A dew bit is something to eat before breakfast, a stay bit something halfway through the morning; a nammit something after lunch; and a crummit something at tea-time.)

Piddletrenthide

THE VILLAGE

The origins of Piddletrenthide go back into the mists of prehistory. Bronze age man probably lived in the valley; he certainly buried his dead there, because some of his barrows or burial mounds are still visible in quite a few fields in the parish. Iron age enclosures are also evident, together with traces of 'Celtic' field systems.

There was also occupation in Roman times. Roman rooftiles and the distinctive Samian pottery have been found around Doles Ash Farm in the east, and a mosaic pavement was discovered in the grounds of the Manor House sometime about 1740. It is still there, covered with earth and grass to preserve both it and the croquet lawn under which it lies. Perhaps a Roman villa stood on the spot. Villas excavated not far away would have relied on the prosperous town of Durnovaria – the Roman Dorchester – with its amphitheatre and aqueduct, for the marketing of their produce, and there is no reason why a villa in Piddletrenthide should not have flourished in the same way.

The first recorded references to Piddletrenthide are in Saxon charters. While the new invaders were conquering the rest of Wessex, the Romano-British population of Dorset managed to keep them at bay for a considerable time. It was not, indeed, until fairly late, probably some time after AD 650 that the marauders finally reached the Dorchester area and even later than that when Saxon rule was finally imposed.

In 891 a charter for the neighbouring settlement of Plush, now a part of Piddletrenthide, defines the village's northern boundary. Seventy-five years later King Edgar ratified to the nuns of Shaftesbury Abbey the possession of ten hides of land at Uppidelen, which must surely refer to Piddletrenthide or at least its upper tithing. Certainly by Saxon times the village was divided into three tithings: the upper, where the church and manor house stand; the middle tithing, where the greater number of houses have been built; and the lower which contains the hamlet of White Lackington. Even today most of the houses are grouped in these three areas, and there is little doubt that by the tenth century at the latest the parish boundaries were the same as they are now. There is a legend, perhaps with more than a grain of truth in it, that Aethelred I, who was King of Wessex in 866 and the elder brother of Alfred the Great, lived in Piddletrenthide, and that such local names as Kingrove and Kingcombe are a reminder of this.

In the year 1002 the Lady Emma, daughter of Richard, Duke of Normandy, became the wife of King Aethelred II, familiarly known as 'the Unready.' Through her marriage she received property in the village of Piddletrenthide, including the church, and in turn she handed it over to the new Benedictine monastery of St Peter at Winchester. Winchester was by now the capital of Wessex – and indeed later rivalled London as the capital of England – and the new monastery had been specially designed for it by Alfred the Great, although it was his son, Edward the Elder, who actually founded it.

Queen Emma was an interesting lady in her own right. Coming as she did from Normandy, she was partly responsible for bringing England under Norman influence and it is quite possible that the bilingual derivation of the name 'Piddletrenthide' is the result of her connection with the village. The allusion is clear: thirty (French *trente*) hides (a measurement of land, said to be enough for one household) on the Piddle, which means nothing more derogatory than a stream of clear water! There are scholars, however, who dispute the French derivation. One of them insists that the word *'trent'* or *'treonta'* comes from the British *'troiient'*, meaning 'a winding river'; another that 'Pyden' is properly a draw-well, from the Latin *'puteus'*, and is also used for 'mire'. No doubt the true derivation will never be finally decided, but to many people it is Queen Emma's connection with the village which is the happiest and most romantic explanation. She did, after all, have two husbands who were kings – after the death of Aethelred she married King Canute – and two sons who were also kings.

The invaluable Domesday book, with its wealth of topographical information, gives a detailed account of Piddletrenthide in the year 1086:

The church of St Peter at Winchester holds Pidrie. Tempus Rex Edwardus [in the time of King Edward] it paid geld for thirty hides. There is land for seventeen ploughs. Of this there are in demesne fifteen hides and two and a half virgates of land [one virgate was thirty acres]and there are five ploughs and twenty serfs and twenty villeins and thirty bordars with eight ploughs. There are three mills rendering 60s. and sixteen acres of meadow. There is pasture two leagues long and half a league wide of the same land. One knight and a certain widow hold three hides and there they have two ploughs. The demesne of the church is worth £28. The rest is worth 40s.

One cannot help speculating about the relationship between the knight and the 'certain widow!'

The statement that 'the church of St Peter at Winchester holds Pidrie' shows that Queen Emma's gift was still helping to swell the coffers of the Benedictines. Twenty-five years later, in the reign of King Henry I, the monastery was removed from its site near the cathedral to a place outside the city walls and re-named Hyde Abbey. The Abbey therefore – most famous as the burial place of Alfred the Great – owned Piddletrenthide and continued to do so until the Dissolution of the Monasteries in the 1530s.

As landlord of the village, Hyde Abbey was also responsible for maintaining a cell or small monastery in the grounds of the mansion which almost certainly stood on the site of the present manor house. It possessed a chapel, dedicated to St Michael, with a chancel, choir, belfry and bells. Two monks, chaplains of the Abbey, were employed to celebrate divine service every day in the house and to distribute alms to the poor. These duties were carried out until the middle of the fourteenth century when for some reason the chapel was dismantled and replaced by a small oratory. This oratory, or part of it, is today used as a farmhouse store in the grounds of the manor house.

The financial status of Piddletrenthide was again recorded in 1288. In that year Pope Nicholas IV granted to King Edward I a tithe – or tenth of the income – from every benefice in the country to help defray the expenses of a crusade to the Holy Land. For this, all towns and villages were valued and 'Trentehude' was deemed to be worth £10, a sum a little higher than the average. No doubt the unfortunate parish priest had to find most, if not all, of the money out of his stipend unless the Abbot of Hyde was generous enough to pay up.

By the time King Henry VIII came to the throne, Piddletrenthide was a thriving community stretching along the bottom of the valley in a linear pattern, although the real centre of village life was a nucleus of dwellings clustered at the foot of the church. This area, together with the lane which runs parallel to the present main road and was once the only route between Piddletrenthide and Dorchester, was and still is known as 'Egypt'. No one seems to know the reason for this name. Perhaps gypsies used to camp thereabouts. A certain museum curator called Mr Toms, who was in the village studying ancient sheepfolds, happened to be near the church during a heavy rainstorm. The water, rushing down through the chalk on to piles of horse-droppings in the lane, ran white and brown.

'Now I know why it is called Egypt,' he said to Harry Hicks, who was with him, 'because it is a land flowing with milk and honey!'

The Reformation, which paved the way for the wholesale dissolution of monasteries great and small, shifted the ownership of many villages all over the country. Piddletrenthide was no exception. The only Dorset manor held by Hyde Abbey, it was now, after the Abbey's dissolution, granted to Winchester College, which remained the principal owner until the 1950s. In their archives are complete lists of the copyholders or tenants of a number of the village houses from the sixteenth century until recent days. It is an odd coincidence that the two largest villages in the Piddle Valley were each owned for hundreds of years by a public school: Piddlehinton by Eton and Piddletrenthide by Winchester.

On 2 May 1654, a fire destroyed twenty-two houses in the village. Help for those made homeless came quickly, initially from the Corporation of Dorchester who next day ordered that, '£5 is to be sent immediately to Pudletrenthead for supply of the necessityes of the poore people whose houses were burnt yesterday.' On 14 May a further £18. 19s. 2d. was sent, the money being collected in the streets of Dorchester. Assistance also came from as far away as Hampshire, Somerset and Wiltshire. It was probably after the fire that the village moved away from the lanes near the church and was rebuilt along what is now the main road.

Fire was a major hazard in those days. In the Overseers' and Churchwardens' Accounts, much of the relief given to villagers and vagabonds was to those 'undon by fire'. On 18 April 1895, it was proposed that a certain John Mitchell be deputed to form a Fire Brigade of ten men, whose wages should be two guineas per annum. Five years later it was agreed by the Parish Council – and no doubt there was a reason for their ruling! – that if the Fire Engine had not been out for the required number of times for practice the men's wages should be cut to one guinea. The engine was housed in a shed next door to Piddletrenthide Mill, and some of the oldest residents can still recall the way in which it chugged up and down the valley. In 1908 there was a fire at Pomeroy's Farm and a claim was sent to the Assurance Offices for £10. Only £3. 9s. 10d. was forthcoming, and this was divided among members of the Brigade and other helpers 'for extinguishing expenses'. The Postmaster of Dorchester agreed that in the case of a fire at night, telegrams might be sent during the hours of darkness to the Constabulary at Dorchester.

During the nineteenth century the population of Piddletrenthide grew, from 449 in 1801 to 680 in 1831. It might have increased further if plans for a canal and even a branch railway line had come to pass. Today there are 382 names on the Electoral Register but the number is increasing as small property developments and 'in-fillings' are carried out. A Baptist chapel, now a dwelling house, was built in White Lackington in 1876, and eighteen years later the Methodist Church was opened. Ralph Wightman has described the church-going habits of the villagers in his father's day: while the Church of England congregation often drove to All Saints in a horse and carriage, the Methodists and Baptists always walked, not because they could not afford transport but because they believed that no one, not even a horse, should work on the Sabbath.

THE CHURCH

All Saints is one of the most beautiful village churches in the whole of Dorset. The tower is as elegant and graceful a one as you could find anywhere, with its pinnacles soaring into the sky and its array of gargoyles carved into grotesque figures, one of which is playing an instrument remarkably like the bagpipes. More ferocious gargoyles, a company of benevolent lions and a crenellated parapet adorn the wall outside the south aisle.

Above the west door of the tower is an inscription in Latin which shows that it was built in the time of Nicholas Locke, the vicar towards the end of the fifteenth century:-
'Est pydeltrenth villa in dorsedie comitatu Nascitur in illa quam rexit Vicariatu 1487' [It is in Piddletrenthide, a town in Dorset where he was born and where he reigns as Vicar 1487]. Dating of a tower is rare, and the engraving of the date is probably the earliest use of Arabic numerals on any building in England.

All Saints has another distinction: it is one of the first churches in the country to be mentioned in a written document. In the year AD 1000 or thereabouts it was recorded that Queen Emma, wife of Aethelred the Unready, gave the village of Piddletrenthide, together with its church, to the monastery at Winchester which later became Hyde Abbey. In spite of this early reference, however, nothing remains of the church that must have stood on the site before the time of the Norman conquest, and only the south doorway and one of the piers of the chancel arch belong to the Norman era. The remainder was built early in the fifteenth century and quite extensively restored 350 years afterwards. A gallery along the west wall against the tower arch was removed during the restoration. An inventory of 1552 mentions five bells in the tower. A sixth was added in 1972 – a treble cast at the famous Whitechapel foundry. The tenor bell, dated 1631, bears a little rhyme:

Com when I call
To serve God all.

The majority of monuments are in memory of the local squires: the Colliers, the Coxes and the Bridges. The most ornate was erected to John Bridge, on the north side of the altar; the oldest is the Purbeck marble slab in the nave just below the chancel step, with a brass inscription which reads: 'here lyethe the bodye of John Colyer whiche departyde this lyfe the firste daye of June in the yere of or. Lorde God MCCCCCLXIIII [1564].' The stained glass is scarcely worthy of so handsome a church, but one window in the south aisle, in memory of Captain G. E. G. Pollard, grandson of the late John E. Bridge, Royal Munster Fusiliers, killed 25 April 1915, is one of the first representations of a man in khaki uniform to appear in church stained glass.

The oak communion table in the south chapel, a fine example of early seventeenth-century woodwork, was at one time removed and lost sight of for many years. Eventually, during the incumbency of the Rev. R. W. H. Dalison (1894–8) it was discovered in the bar of a public house in the village and brought back to the church to serve its original purpose.

The roll of vicars dates from 1301 and is unbroken except for the years of the Civil War, when the then vicar, Thomas Colnet, was accused of deserting his parish, and at least three men, John Paynel, Benjamin Walters and Benjamin Maber served as clerks or ministers until Maber was formally presented to the living in November 1657. James Hicks (1845–88) has an important place in the church's history; he was responsible for the considerable restoration completed during the period, the work being carried out by his brother, John, who later took the young Thomas Hardy as his apprentice. The next incumbent but one, the Rev. Roger Dalison, also has his claim to fame: a young relative of his often used to spend his school holidays in the vicarage. The boy was called Bernard Montgomery and he was later to become the most distinguished soldier of the Second World War. There was, too, the Rev. C. W. H. Dicker (1905–13) a local historian and not inconsiderable painter, whose life came to a tragic end when he was setting off for a holiday on his motorcycle. At the end of Swan Lane, his cycle skidded and he was flung off into the path of a steam milk lorry and instantly killed.

Older parishioners still remember the pageant which Mr Dicker organized in the grounds of the vicarage in 1910, with stands erected to seat 400 spectators. Starting with the Stone Age, the vicar devised scenes from Dorset history down the ages, with a prologue by Mr Stevens, a shepherd in his smock, singing a song whose refrain ran:-

Ye may seek a land like Dorset
But ye'll never come across it
Though ye seek the wide world through
From the Nothe to Timbuctoo.

The churchyard has its own interesting features. Under the north wall a memorial states: 'Here lies the body of an unknown man found dead on an adjoining hill after a snow-storm.' The man was found on Cerne Hill and buried in Piddletrenthide churchyard, and no one ever discovered who he was or where he came from. There are two rounded tombstones, slightly askew on the south-east side of the churchyard, both dated 1616, in memory of two members of the Dumberfield family, the name which Hardy adapted for his most famous fictional family, the d'Urbervilles. And Ralph Wightman, the well-known author and broadcaster, whose nephew and niece still live in the Valley, is buried in the south-west corner of the churchyard.

THE ALTAR STONE

In the centre of Piddletrenthide a house contains a relic which has been the subject of discussion and speculation by many archaeologists and historians and whose existence may well go back to the days of King Henry VII.

Pear Tree Cottage – and there actually is a pear tree trained elegantly across the wall which fronts the main street – is one of the oldest and most attractive houses in the village. It originally belonged, as did the rest of Piddletrenthide, to Hyde Abbey in Winchester, and there is a written record of two cottages, almost certainly semi-detached, on the site as early as 1506. It is not possible to say how long before that date they were built, but the stone and flint construction of the ground floor, exactly like that of other authentically dated buildings, makes it almost certain that Pear Tree Cottage in some form or other has existed for well over 500 years.

During the last war, a German pilot, looking for Piddlehinton Army Camp and chased by night fighters, jettisoned his bombs over Piddletrenthide. One fell on the end of the butcher's shop, demolishing part of it and damaging the cottage. According to Bill Hunt, the whole block was moved two inches down the road by the blast. Considerable damage was done to Pear Tree Cottage, particularly to the eastern wall, and Bill Park and his bricklayer, Bill Hunt, were employed to carry out repairs. During the work of demolition and rebuilding, with flint and stone cleverly chosen to match the existing walls, there was discovered a large object made apparently of Portland Stone, in Bill Hunt's words 'the size of a big table and hollowed out smooth as smooth.' To him it looked for all the world like an ancient font. Unfortunately, Bill Park, not realizing the significance of the find, took it away with him, broke it up and used it to build a wall.

Some ten years later the cottage was sold and the new owners, Mr and Mrs Cecil Matthews, decided on some alterations. One of the first things to be done was to dismantle an unsightly grate in the dining-room. The plaster was removed and a second discovery, even more interesting, was made. Hidden by the plaster and now exposed to the light of day for the first time in perhaps hundreds of years, was a huge slab of stone with five crosses engraved, one in each corner and a fifth in the middle, the whole thing wedged beneath the massive oak beam which formed the lintel of the now open fireplace. There seems little doubt that the slab is an altar stone, although the fifth cross in the centre is a mystery in itself. Most altar stones of the same type are carved with four crosses, one in each corner. A fifth cross is traditionally supposed to imply that the altar has been consecrated twice: in other words, removed from a holy place and then reconsecrated.

So where did the altar stone come from, and why was it in Pear Tree Cottage? Again Bill Hunt has a theory. He believes that in the Middle Ages the cottage may have been a hostel or resting-place for monks on their travels between Milton Abbas and Cerne Abbas. West of Milton Abbas there is an ancient and now derelict pulpit-church at Lyscombe. There may well have been a little chapel in Piddletrenthide Church, behind where the organ now is, because we know of the will of a certain Alex Riston of 1392 requesting to be buried in the Holy Trinity Chapel of the church. Milton Abbas and Lyscombe, Lyscombe and Piddletrenthide, Piddletrenthide and Cerne Abbas are more or less in a straight line. What more likely than that the journeying monks, making their pilgrimages to the holy places, rested at Pear Tree Cottage and said their prayers before the altar stone?

There is a second possibility. When Hyde Abbey became the landlord of Piddletrenthide, it was responsible for the building and maintenance of a monks' cell in the grounds of the manor house, together with a small chapel. This was dismantled sometime in the middle of the fourteenth century. It needs little imagination to visualize the ruins of the chantry – a heap of broken stones, an altar slab, maybe even a font – lying neglected and forgotten on the grass and then being rescued by someone who wished to build a monks' hostel on the pilgrim way to Cerne. It is even possible that when the little chapel in the manor grounds was dismantled the holy objects were taken straight to what is now Pear

Tree Cottage and reassembled and reconsecrated there. And then, later on when the monasteries were dissolved and the monks were no longer able to wander at will along the Dorset lanes, the hostel became an ordinary dwelling house and the altar stone hidden for another 400 years. It is all speculation of course. But the very existence of such a venerable object evokes an atmosphere of romance and mystery.

PIDDLETRENTHIDE VILLAGE SCHOOL

In his will of 1746, a certain John Harding of Piddletrenthide directed that the sale of his property in the county of Somerset was to be used to provide a schoolmaster for the poor boys of the parish. A survey of the village, made in the 1770s and now in the archives of Winchester College, shows a school and a poor house on the site where the school now stands. The present building was erected in 1848 by the descendants of John Bridge, one-time lord of the manor, in recognition of his contribution to the life and well-being of the village. A terracotta bust of the benefactor stands in the main schoolroom, with a brass plate underneath it bearing the inscription:

This bust is placed here to record the memory of John Bridge, Esq., who during a period of more than fifty years residence in London never forgot this his native village and it is in compliance with his well-known wishes that this schoolhouse has been erected at the expense of his grateful descendants. 1848. The land contributed by John Gawler Bridge. The funds for building given by Amelia and Maria Bridge.

Amelia and Maria were John Bridge's daughters and John Gawler Bridge his nephew, a partner in his uncle's business and at one time Groom of the great Chamber to both King William IV and Queen Victoria. The bust itself was carved by E. H. Bailey, RA, who was responsible for the reliefs on the Marble Arch in London and also for the statue of Nelson in Trafalgar Square.

The following extracts from the School Log Book, written by a succession of head teachers, give a vivid picture both of the school and its pupils and of the social life of the time.

30 July 1862 [the first year when records were kept]:
The school hours as usual. A gentleman's shirt was finished by a girl of eleven years for which she gained a prize at the exhibition of the Dorset Society for the improvement of the condition of the labouring classes.

9 and 10 March 1863:
Mrs Brooks called to arrange about the banners, favours and medals which were to be carried by the children on the 10th. This being a special holiday to celebrate the marriage of the Prince of Wales, it was observed as such. The schoolroom was used in the evening for the entertainment at dinner of the aged poor of the parish.

7 October 1863:
A boy stood in middle of room for half-an-hour for breaking a nut during a lesson.

6 June 1865:
Mr Bridge has returned the school registers and examination schedule which he took away last night having found several of the numbers wrong in the schedule. This is the first time a figure has been wrong in any account, register or schedule during the time I have been in charge of the school and the reason is that at other times I have had a child to help me but this year owing to the long winter and sudden spring the older children have been wanted after school either to help in the gardens or to get supper for their parents. The preparing of needlework occupies the whole evening and the books were made up and the schedule filled during the night when my eyes often became glazed from fatigue and candle light.

4 September:
The harvest still being unfinished and so many children being engaged in gleaning and picking potatoes, the school will not open until 11 September.

7 March 1866:
The Fast for the Cattle Plague. Most of the children attended Church with their parents.

24 April:
Two children lately admitted were withdrawn on being required to sweep the schoolroom.

16 September 1868:
Dorchester Fair and the Fox-hunting drew away many of the children today.

11 November 1869:
On account of the severe cold the children spent more time than usual in singing and dancing.

15 March 1870:
First class did a scripture lesson for Rev. Bigg. Had to reprove both teachers for repeated neglect of lessons.

20 July:
Very few children here in the morning and only one in the afternoon due to the Temperance Fete.

17 October:
M. Hillier again late for lessons which were as usual disgracefully prepared. Have warned her so repeatedly, that I shall be obliged, now, to express to Mr Bridge my conviction that her carelessness or indolence unfit her for the duties of a teacher.

14 February 1871:
Mr Bridge reported that a complaint had been made to him that a little boy, Archelaus House, had been punished too severely. Mr Bridge wishes punishment by badges expressive of disgrace to supersede, as far as possible, corporal punishment.

28 October 1874:
A monitor appointed this day at two shillings per week.

23 May 1879:
Some of the little ones, who have been home nearly all the winter, have come to school again.

11 March 1881:
The Rev. J. Hicks [Vicar of Piddletrenthide] visited the school yesterday and reproved some boys for their misconduct out of school. Richard Slade was expelled for writing indecent words in the school books and for using bad language out of school.

28 September 1883:
The Rev. R. V. Thompson came in for a short time yesterday and said he met two boys in the street who told him they were absent from school because they were pig-keeping.

18 June 1886:
Mr Bridge distributed money to all those who had made over 300 attendances during the past year. Forty-one scholars received sums varying from ½d. to 2s. 4½d.

24 June 1887:
The school closed on two days in honour of the Queen's Jubilee.

25 August 1893:
The numbers are ridiculously low for the numbers on books. 22 children have not yet put in an appearance since the holidays. Progress is very seriously hindered by this in addition to being heavily handicapped through lack of intelligence.

29 January 1894:
Ellis punished at noon. This is the first time a cane has been used in this school for over a year.

27 February:
The school was closed to-day the master having to attend Cerne Petty Sessions for punishing Ellis on Jan. 29th. Took the teachers and some of the scholars. Without hearing any evidence whatever for the defence the bench dismissed the case.

2 June:
A false report that some newly admitted children were suffering from itch disease has made havoc with attendance.

1 February 1895:
The children are very backward. Standard III and upwards until my arrival could not repeat six lines of their poetry, geography and grammar were scarcely commenced for the year and even in class I the children count on their fingers and do not know with any certainty the multiplication tables. Neither do they know the tune or words of a single song.

24 June:
Admitted Mable Downton and Annie Harwood. This latter is a girl of 9½ years of age, she knows about a dozen words as: it, is, to, etc. She cannot do any sums and her writing is on a par with her other attainments. She is a poor neglected girl and I see no other place for her than the first standard, as she is much too 'big' for the infants.

5 March 1897:
Frank Addams from the 'Band of Hope' gave a model lesson to the upper room scholars, the aim being to show the evil effects of alcohol on the human system.

22 June:
Whole day holiday – Diamond Jubilee of Queen Victoria.

25 June:
A thin attendance all the week probably caused in a great measure by the excitement over the Jubilee celebrations, etc. etc.

23 September 1898:
Sent a request to the Managers asking them to re-engage Norah House who was formally [*sic*] assistant here. The Managers felt they were unable to pay the amount (£20 per annum) asked by her.

27 April 1900:
Commenced teaching a patriotic song, 'The Glorious Flag of England'.

25 May:
Commenced teaching the children the song, 'Soldiers of the Queen'.

1 June:
A tea was given to the children by J. Barkworth, Esq., to commemorate the Relief of Mafeking.

23 January 1901:
Queen Victoria died last evening.

1 November:
The attendance is still affected by potato-picking which this week has been assisted with colds.

2 June 1902:
[in red ink] Information to hand this morning that peace is declared [this was the end of the Boer War].

16 October:
The Vicar visited the Master to ask him for an explanation as to his irregularity of attendance at Church, and to inform him that under the Trust Deed, he, the Vicar, was *solely* responsible for the religious and moral instruction of the children.

16 June 1911:
Closed school for week – Coronation. [King George V and Queen Mary].

24 July 1913:
Two boys, Kenneth Wightman and Ralph Wightman, have gained the County Agricultural Scholarships. [The latter was to become the well-known writer and broadcaster].

26 November 1914:
24 children took part in a patriotic concert in aid of the Belgians.

16 November 1915:
The upper children made and sold about 400 Russian flags.

22 May 1916:
The Daylight Saving Bill came into force this morning and school opened at the 'new' 9 o'clock.

24 May:
To-day is 'Empire Day'. Ordinary lessons were not taken and at 11 o'clock the children marched into the play-ground where an address was given to them by the Vicar. They then sang patriotic songs, 'The Union Jack' etc. to an audience of parents and friends and a party of wounded soldiers from the Convalescent Home here [at the Manor]. The large 'Union Jack' presented to the school by Major de Heriez Smith was hoisted for the first time on the flag staff given by H. Barkworth Esq.

18 January 1917:
This afternoon one child, Marian Payne, came to school with her hair hanging loose. She said her mother had combed it, but had not time to plait it. One of the teachers plaited it and tied it for her. At playtime her father came into the school, and took her away, saying he did not care for anybody's authority, he would not have her hair plaited.

5 June:
I have received acknowledgments of receipt of 7 dozen eggs collected by the children for our Dorchester Hospitals.

6 March 1918:
The 1st class had a lesson on filling up the 'Meat Cards'.

31 October:
The total quantity of blackberries sent from this School for Government use is 2694 lbs.

15 May 1924:
The Vicar gave an interesting account of what he had seen at the Wembley Exhibition.

6 July 1925:
'Summer Time' is having its usual bad effect on all the classes.

1 May 1930:
A party of girls was taken to see Princess Mary at the Guide Rally.

13 September 1935:
First immunisation against Diptheria took place to-day.

30 September 1938:
Children were fitted with gas masks to-day.

7 September 1939:
Because of the outbreak of war, opening after Summer Holiday was postponed until to-day. Several evacuees admitted.

1 July 1940:
23 evacuees and their teacher were admitted. The air-raid alarm went several times this week.

28 October 1941:
School dinners, brought from the Dorchester Canteen by W. V. S. workers, started to-day.

15 December 1943:
Two American officers called, inviting children and staff to a Christmas Party at Piddlehinton Camp.

3 May 1944:
.Two Plush boys absent to-day after being injured last evening by the explosion of ammunition with which they were playing. Both boys are in hospital. A.R.P. authorities notified.

9 May:
The Senior A.R.P. warden conducted an air-raid practice.

8 May 1945:
V. E. Day. School closed until Thursday.

11 May:
School Thanksgiving Service.

8 September 1946:
We re-opened as a Primary School. 35 now on books.

The School Song

In 1943, the senior class composed a school song which was subsequently printed in the Dorset Year Book of 1948 to celebrate the school's centenary:

> Through the vale of Pydeltrenthide
> Gently flows the River Trent,
> Ancient trees the hillside cover;
> Here our childhood days are spent.
> *REFRAIN:*
> *Sing a song of Pydeltrenthide!*
> *Though the years may bear you far,*
> *Keep in mind the good old motto:*
> *'HITCH YOUR WAGON TO A STAR!'*
>
> Day by day the feet of children
> Enter through the playground gate,
> Coming to the village schoolroom
> Built in eighteen forty eight.
> *REFRAIN:*
>
> Farmers' sons and farmers' daughters,
> Butchers', bakers' families,
> Children of the groom and blacksmith
> Here may learn the way to please.
> *REFRAIN:*
>
> Here we learn to train our bodies,
> Finding health and self-control,
> Cultivate our mental powers
> And prepare for Heav'n our soul.
> *REFRAIN:*

The School Gates

The wrought-iron gates through which for over 130 years hundreds of children have made their way to school have an unusual history. For them the village and the school are once again indebted to John Bridge, for it was he who brought them to Piddletrenthide and added them to his collection of curios at the Manor House.

In the year 1820 or thereabouts a certain Samuel Tansley, the Westminster Abbey blacksmith, removed all the railings that had then protected the royal tombs from prying fingers. No one knows precisely why he did this or who gave him permission. It is possible that the railings were removed in order to give more room for the guests and other sightseers at the coronation of King George IV. Or maybe the Abbey architect, Wyatt, took a dislike to them and gave his instructions to the mason, Gayfere, who in turn allowed Tansley to remove them and make what use of them he wished.

Whosoever's authority he acted upon, twenty years later Tansley admitted that he had bought all the railings in order to re-use them for his own wrought-iron work. He further agreed that he had sold some of them – in particular those which had surrounded the tombs of Mary, Queen of Scots, the Lady Margaret Beaufort and the Countess of Lennox – to Mr Bridge, of the firm of Rundell and Bridge on Ludgate Hill.

So John Bridge, with an eye to increasing his collection of trophies, brought the railings to Piddletrenthide and placed them in the Manor House, and no doubt they were a source of great satisfaction to him. There they remained for over a decade until Bridge died. Fourteen years after that, in 1848, the village school was built.

Amelia and Maria Bridge were anxious to make the new school a building worthy of their father's memory. There, cluttering up the Manor, were three sets of elegant and historic railings. What more suitable decision could there be than that one set should be used to grace the memorial, should become, in fact, the school gates? And so it hap-

pened. In due time two gates, with their 'thirteen dia-
gonally-set spearheaded uprights joined by horizontal rails,
and a broad top rail with cable mouldings above and below a
row of lozenge-shaped jewels,' were placed at the entrance
to the school. There they remain to this day.

The question has yet to be answered: from which tomb
did they come? For a long time the Scots Queen was the
favourite contender. She was, after all, the most famous
and most glamorous of the three. Lady Margaret Beaufort
had her adherents, too. Also known as the Countess of
Richmond, she was the mother of King Henry VII and,
besides having founded the Cambridge colleges of St John's
and Christ's, was the founder of Wimborne Grammar
School. It would in a way be appropriate to think that her
railings were gracing another Dorset school.

But there is well-nigh incontrovertible evidence that
neither of these celebrated ladies has lost the railings of her
tomb. In 1911, sixty years after the railings left Westminster
Abbey for Piddletrenthide, there was a sale of the Bridge
collection. And among the lots set down in Messrs. Waring
and Gillow's catalogue were two significant ones. Lot 357
consisted of 'an interesting "Stuart" relic, in the form of
wrought iron railings, with scroll hanging for tomb lamp,
which formed the grave surround of Mary Queen of Scots,
and was removed from Peterborough Cathedral, on the
occasion of the body of Mary Queen of Scots being conveyed to Westminster Abbey by command of her son,
James I. This was purchased by Mr John Bridge, July 1826.'
Lot 358 was described as 'another early fifteenth century
relic in the form of a wrought iron grave surround of
Margaret, Countess of Richmond, mother of King Henry
the Seventh.' There were also various lots of 'old iron' and
'iron gratings' lying out in the hay fields and grounds of the
Manor which do not concern this story, although it is quite
possible that they, too, came from the Abbey, if not from
any royal tomb.

It seems pretty certain, therefore, that the two sets of
railings advertised in the auctioneers' catalogue were those
of Mary, Queen of Scots, and the Lady Margaret Beaufort.
At all events, they were bought by a well-known art dealer

and subsequently sold by him to the National Art Collections Fund, who returned them to the Abbey. The sum mentioned for the purchase of each set was £400.

So that leaves the third tomb, that of Margaret Douglas, Countess of Lennox, whose railings must surely be the final set that John Bridge brought down to his Dorset home. And who was she?

Her mother was Margaret Tudor, Princess of England and elder sister of King Henry VII, her father Archibald Douglas, Earl of Angus, the man whom the Princess married after the death of her first husband, King James IV of Scotland. Her son was Henry Stuart, Lord Darnley, wretched one-time husband of Mary, Queen of Scots. In Westminster Abbey, her tomb, bereft of rails, in the chapel which she shares with her ill-fated daughter-in-law, announces in grandiloquent terms her noble lineage:

This lady had to her great grandfather King Edward IV, to her grandfather King Henry VII, to her uncle King Henry VIII, to her cousin german King Edward VI, to her brother King James V of Scotland, to her son King Henry I, to her grandchild King James VI, having to her great grandmother and grandmother two queens both named Elizabeth, to her mother Margaret, Queen of Scots, to her aunt Mary, the French Queen, to her cousins german Mary and Elizabeth, Queens of England, to her niece and daughter-in-law Mary, Queen of Scots.

So it seems evident that the tomb of a very great lady, whose ancestors and descendants have woven many vivid threads into the tapestry of England's history, provided the railings which for over 130 years have formed the gates of Piddletenthide School. There are those who say they should be returned to Westminster Abbey. Others consider that Dorchester Museum might be a more suitable home for them. But the villagers of Piddletrenthide will not lightly or willingly surrender one of their most prized possessions.

Piddlehinton School

Piddlehinton also has a village school, with a history no doubt as rich in social commentary as that to be found in the Piddletrenthide School Log Book. Unfortunately, with a love of tidiness apparently greater than a love of history, a headmistress in the 1950s destroyed all the records, even those concerning the time when Thomas Hardy's sister, Mary, was teaching in the school.

ROYAL CONNECTIONS

There is a connection, albeit a tenuous one, between the quiet valley of the River Piddle, even quieter in the first decades of the last century, and the frenzied, flamboyant, extravagant court of George III and George IV. The link, once again, is that most interesting of Valley personalities, John Bridge.

Bridge's parents, Thomas and Mary, lived for a time at South House, Piddletrenthide, and their memorial, in carved profile, can be seen in the north aisle of the church. In 1812 John, then fifty-seven years old, bought the copyhold of the Manor House from Winchester College and so became the lord of the manor. His London house was in Shepherd's Bush and he spent most of his time there, but he never lost interest in his Dorset country home and enriched it with many of his treasures.

John Bridge and his colleague, Philip Rundell, had started their business lives as shop assistants in the firm which was later to bear their name; by the time John had become the lord of the manor of Piddletrenthide, Rundell and Bridge were probably the most celebrated jewellers and silversmiths of their day. Their shop on Ludgate Hill was patronized not only by members of high society but also by the King himself and the royal family. In his memoirs, Philip Rundell explains that it was always his partner who was deputed to negotiate with King George III and the Prince Regent and that 'in consequence of his unassuming demeanour and condescending manners, he became a great favourite with King George the Third and his royal consort, and all the Princesses, who were in the habit of consulting Mr Bridge upon all occasions, when a change of, or an alteration in, the setting of their jewellery was deemed expedient.'

Rundell goes on to say that 'his present Majesty [King George IV] . . . has been equally condescending with respect to Mr Bridge who has, in numerous instances, been honoured by conduct on the part of his sovereign that bordered somewhat on familiarity: a mark of favour not very common on the part of the King.'

The King's condescension is not altogether surprising. During the time when he was Prince Regent he owed Rundell and Bridge thousands of pounds. His well-known extravagance and the gifts which he lavished on his favourites meant that he could not pay. And in due course many royal items of jewellery and plate found their way into John Bridge's collection in part-payment of the massive royal debts.

It happened that on one occasion the shop on Ludgate Hill was visited by one of the royal princes: history does not relate which one of the five. Bridge happened to be away at the time and so Rundell had perforce to deal with his royal patron.

The Prince looked round at the rich display and said with envy in his voice:

'You must be a very rich man, Mr Rundell.'

'Quite the reverse, your Highness,' retorted Rundell, 'since nobody thinks of paying what he owes, which keeps me poor. If we could collect our just debts then indeed we might be rich.'

The Prince looked thoughtful. He owed the firm a great deal. Then, after a moment's silence, he requested Rundell to send Mr Bridge to him the following morning. John Bridge did as he was asked, and a cheque for £500 was handed to him to put towards the Prince's account and so pay off some of his debts.

'There you are,' said Rundell triumphantly. 'I am convinced the Royal Dukes would pay *if properly rubbed up!*'

While he was still Prince Regent, George IV commissioned from Rundell and Bridge a collection of plate which came to be known as 'The Prince's Plate'. This the firm put on display with other spectacular items and so the shop became 'a fashionable place of resort for the higher circles.' The publicity could do the firm no harm: the members of grand society who flocked to see the exquisite pieces stayed to buy trinkets and other jewellery that caught their eye and this amply compensated the partners for the trouble entailed in showing the visitors round.

Rundell died in 1827 and his partner seven years later, but already John Bridge's nephew, John Gawler Bridge, had entered the firm. His connection with the royal family continued after his uncle's death and indeed has persisted in a manner of speaking until the present day. The Imperial Crown made for the coronation of King George IV and worn also by King William IV was unsuitable for Queen Victoria. No doubt it was far too big. Accordingly, John Gawler Bridge fashioned for her a new 'Crown of State', using jewels from the Imperial Crown, including the famous ruby of the Black Prince worn by King Henry V at the Battle of Agincourt and a sapphire said to have come from a ring belonging to Edward the Confessor. The cost of the job was £1000. This crown is still worn by the sovereign on important occasions, such as the opening of parliament, and the link between the monarch and the Bridges of Piddletrenthide maintained.

Like his uncle, John Gawler Bridge believed in publicity. He was also very proud of his crown. And so just before the coronation he displayed it in the shop on Ludgate Hill, as the Prince's Plate had been exhibited before, and again all the fashionable world thronged to see it, so many that police had to be drafted in to control the crowds.

But not everyone approved of the exhibition. There was a certain Mr Swift who was Keeper of the Jewel House in the Tower of London. He had no salary but lived on the entrance fees paid by visitors to see the Crown Jewels. He was expecting a good return from those who wished to gaze upon the new crown, but Bridge had beaten him to it. Swift complained to the Lord Chamberlain that there would be nobody left to see the crown when eventually it arrived in the Jewel House, and that every visitor to Ludgate Hill deprived him of the shilling he would have charged in the Tower. But Bridge retorted that his exhibition would serve only to whet the public appetite for further inspection of his marvellous work of art. The Lord Chamberlain agreed with him. And with that the Jewel House Keeper had to be content.

'THE GENERAL'

One of Piddletrenthide's most celebrated and best loved residents was General Sir Henry Jackson, KCB, CMG, DSO, DL, who lived at West House for over thirty-five years and died in 1972 aged ninty-three.

In the first world war he was mentioned in despatches no less than eight times, and at the end of it had become the youngest Major-General in the British Army. In 1919 he accompanied General Rawlinson to north Russia to help organize the evacuation of British troops from Archangel and Murmansk before they became frozen in for the winter. During the second world war at the age of sixty he was put in command of the Southern Area of the Local Defence Volunteers, later to become the Home Guard. Once he was instructing his men in the use of the home-made grenade known as the 'Molotov cocktail' and in the use of the flare. He threw out a flare and suddenly realized it was a Molotov cocktail. He shouted to his men to get down and they all fell to the ground. When the noise of the explosion had died down, not a leaf was left on the surrounding trees.

During the war, the General also used to have homing pigeons coming back to a little cowhouse in the grounds of West House. It was an important and very secret affair, because the birds brought back reports from the Free French Underground Movement and after they had arrived word was sent to the War Office and a despatch rider would come down to take back the coded messages. To train the pigeons, General Jackson would put his enormous hunter, of over seventeen hands, between the shafts of the village hearse and in this way take the birds out into the country to release them. As they became more and more proficient at finding their way home he would drive the hearse further and further away.

One of Genneral Jackson's great interests was the Boy Scout movement, and nothing pleased him more than to have scouts camping in his grounds. On his ninetieth birthday he held a garden party for his village friends and for the farming supporters of the Cattistock Hunt, for he was a keen rider to hounds even after reaching an advanced age. The cake at the party was cut with a sword which had previously been used at the Battle of Dettingen in 1743, the last engagement in which a king of England led his troops into action. He greeted each of his guests in turn and was on his feet throughout the afternoon. After an hour's rest he was up and about again, this time to welcome another 200 friends from all over Dorset. He dearly loved a party and on this occasion he had managed to have two! The General lies in Piddletrenthide churchyard and is also commemorated in a tablet set inside the west wall of the church. His mongrel dog, Dorset, of whom he was very fond, is buried in a field behind West House, with a little headstone to mark the spot.

PASSENGER ON THE *TITANIC*

Mr Barkworth, who lived at South House for many years, had a brother called Algie who was a passenger on the *Titanic*. He was one of the lucky ones to be saved. When he came back to Piddletrenthide he told Harry Hicks, whose father worked for Mr Barkworth:
'When I reached Southampton and saw the ship, I said: "That ship is too big to float." When she struck the iceberg I was sitting in the lounge. I knew at once that something dreadful had happened and so I ran to my cabin, put my belongings in a case and went up on deck. The ship gave a lurch. I had always understood that before sinking, ships gave just such a lurch, so I pulled off my coat, flung my case in the sea and jumped in after it. I was sucked down and down and it seemed a life-time before I surfaced. I swam for a long, long time and then found a bit of wreckage and clung to it until at last I was picked up by one of the rescue craft.'
Algie Barkworth's home was in Yorkshire, and he told Harry Hicks:
'Before I left, I locked every door and drawer in the house. Now I have lost all my keys and so when I get home I shall have to advertise for an expert burglar to open it all!'

KIDDLES FARM

Twenty years ago an advertisement appeared in the magazine *Country Life:*

> Dorset – 8 miles Dorchester
> In the valley of the River Piddle
> Kiddles Farm, Piddletrenthide
> A Small Mixed Farm
> With Small Period Farmhouse
> Dining/Living Room, Kitchen
> 3 Bedrooms, Bathroom

This inspired the celebrated American poet and humorist, Ogden Nash, to write the following:

Paradise for Sale

Had I the shillings, pounds and pence,
I'd pull up stakes and hie me hence;
I'd buy that small mixed farm in Dorset,
Which has an inglenook and faucet –
Kiddles Farm,
Piddletrenthide,
In the valley of the River Piddle.

I'd quit these vehement environs
Of diesel fumes and horns and sirens,
This manic, fulminating ruction
Of demolition and construction,
For Kiddles Farm,
Piddletrenthide,
In the valley of the River Piddle.

Yes, quit for quietude seraphic
Con Edison's embrangled traffic,
To sit reflecting that the skylark,
Which once was Shelley's, now is my lark,
At Kiddles Farm,
Piddletrenthide,
In the valley of the River Piddle.

I'm sure the gods could not but bless
The man who lives at that address,
And revenue agents would wash their hands
And cease to forward their demands
To Kiddles Farm,
Piddletrenthide,
In the valley of the River Piddle.

Oh, the fiddles I'd fiddle,
The riddles I'd riddle,
The skittles I'd scatter,
The winks I would tiddle!
Then hey diddle diddle!
I'll jump from the griddle
And live out my days
To the end from the middle
On Kiddles Farm,
Piddletrenthide,
In the valley of the River Piddle.

General Sir Henry Jackson, who was living in West House, Piddletrenthide, at the time, wrote to the poet expressing his delight at the verses and hoping that Ogden Nash might one day be able to visit the source of his inspiration. He received this reply:

Dear Sir,
  I am most grateful for your letter, as it gives me both pride and pleasure to learn that my verses have been read and not disliked in Piddletrenthide. I particularly appreciate your own kind words and those of the Messrs Syme, and I hope that good fortune will before too long allow me to accept your invitation.
                    Sincerely yours,
                    Ogden Nash

A further letter from Nash went on to say:

  . . . You might be interested to hear that I've had more letters about this particular poem than on anything I have ever done;

letters from both English and American lovers of Piddletrenthide and its surroundings. Their enthusiasm is highly infectious and I hope I will be able before too long to come and see for myself the countryside which has so enchanted me.

Please accept my belated good wishes on your 80th birthday.

Sincerely yours,

Ogden Nash

Ogden Nash lived twelve years after he wrote the second letter, but history does not relate that he ever set foot in the Piddle Valley.

The sale of Kiddles Farm brought to an end a long tenancy. The two Symes brothers, well-known sheep farmers in the Valley, were through their mother direct descendants of the Kiddle family, who had been tenants of the farm for nearly 400 years, almost all the time as tenants of. Winchester College. Although the connection is now broken, the name of the Kiddle family will always be perpetuated by the name of the farm and of 'Kiddles Bottom' on the Ordnance Survey map.

Harry Hawker, whose daughter-in-law and grandson still live in Piddletrenthide, was the carrier who used to drive first the horse van and later the omnibus from Dorchester through the Valley. On the journey he would shout out the names of the stopping places to his passengers. One foggy night he drew up outside the European Inn in Piddletrenthide.

'Where we be now, Mr Hawker?' asked an old lady.

'European, Ma'am,' he answered, looking down the bus at her.

'That I b'aint,' she protested indignantly. 'It's only the drops off me umbrella!'

(The European, although its title sounds surprisingly modern, is thought to have been given its name at the time of the Napoleonic Wars.)

Poem and letters reproduced by kind permission of Messrs J. M. Dent & Sons Ltd.

Alton St Pancras

THE VILLAGE AND THE CHURCH

Alton St Pancras has the distinction of housing the source of the River Piddle, a fact commemorated in its Anglo-Saxon name, which means the homestead ('*ton*') at the source ('*awiell*'). Clearly there has been a settlement here from Saxon days, but Celtic field systems and tumuli in the surrounding fields show that people lived here long before the coming of the Dark Ages.

Alton is the northernmost of the Piddle Valley villages, a ribbon development of houses scattered here and there along the valley bottom with hills sloping gently up on either side. The soil is chalk with flints and stones, as any gardener will feelingly tell you.

Now, as at the time of the Domesday Book, the sole industry is agriculture: dairy farming for the most part with some arable. Sheep have been kept here in the past, as in the rest of the Valley, but not any more. There are four farms; running from north to south these are Alton Common, Barcombe (incorporating Holcombe Dairy Farm), Austral and Alton Mill, the last reminding us that from Domesday until quite recently the village also boasted a mill. These apart, we are purely residential. The school closed in the

1930s, the general store and Post Office in 1977. Both buildings are now private houses, as is also the former vicarage since the parish of St Pancras was combined with the other Piddle Valley parishes.

There is some disagreement as to the actual source of the River Piddle. Some say that it rises in the grounds of the Manor, in a spinney appropriately named Soggy Wood, others that it is further north at the start of the road leading to Holcombe Dairy Farm. Whichever it is, the two streams merge outside Austral Farm and from that point flow southward as one.

The hub of the village, in so far as there is one, is the Pinnacles, the stone gateway leading jointly to the Manor, the church and Austral Farm. The Manor was 'modernized' in Georgian times by its then owner, Thomas Haskett, who lies buried in the chancel of the church, although the structure of the house is much older. Austral House is also eighteenth century and many of its outbuildings, like those of Barcombe Farm, are of the traditional design of flint banded with red brick. Barcombe Farm still has a forge where an itinerant blacksmith would come twice a week to shoe horses and repair farm machinery. Also in traditional vein are several thatched cottages of Dorset cob scattered throughout the village.

The church has a fifteenth-century tower, a Norman north doorway and a thirteenth-century coffin-lid which acts as the inner lintel to the west door, but otherwise it is comparatively modern, dating from extensive rebuilding in 1874. The font is Perpendicular and on the chancel step rests a rare relic of medieval days: a cresset stone. This is a block of stone with nine cup-shaped hollows in which oil was burned to give light; it was found quite by chance by the present Vicar only three years ago. He detected it leaning, bottom side up, against the vestry door where it had probably been used for centuries as a door stop without anyone realizing its value. The most striking features of an otherwise modest building are two modern stained-glass windows, one in naturalistic style showing St Francis preaching to the birds and the other a symbolic design in muted shades of grey, red and gold.

The church's dedication to St Pancras causes some confusion, as there were two St Pancrases, one a first-century bishop and the other a fourth-century boy, and Lambeth Palace is uncertain as to which is our dedicatee. However, local opinion comes down firmly in favour of the boy: indeed, patronal festival services have been held in honour of his feast day on 12 May. He was a Phrygian orphan, taken by his uncle to Rome, where they were both converted to Christianity and martyred by the Emperor Diocletian when Pancras was only fourteen. He became the patron saint of children and was very popular for some years after his martyrdom, particularly in England, although for centuries now his fame has been eclipsed by that of St Nicholas, more familiarly known as Santa Claus.

Three hundred years ago, the conduct of the St Pancras congregation was evidently not as exemplary as it is today. The Churchwardens' Presentments contain lurid reports of alehouse brawls, drunkenness and bibulous revels even inside the church itself. In 1671, for instance, a certain Henry Spinter was accused of being drunk during divine service and it was said of him that

one Saboth daye a littel before the eveninge prayer he went up into the tower and at a trappe dore did pisse downe upon theare heads in the belfry that they could not stand there nor neare itt to the great offence of those that were present."

The parson himself was not exempt from criticism, one vicar in the year 1608 being reprimanded by his churchwardens for regularly riding to the near-by village of Chesilborne 'to footeball upon the sabbothe day.'

As in the other Valley churches, the accounts give detailed evidence of money spent on the upkeep of the church. The record of one complete year serves as an example:

An Account of Money Expended by Thos. Henning Churchwarden from
Easter 1815 to Easter 1816

		£	s.	d.
Paid	The Clerks wages	2	0	0
	For Bread and Wine	1	4	8
	For the Plumber's Work		11	0
	For mending the Surplices		1	2
	For a Hair Brush		3	0
	For do.		1	1
	For a Mop		2	0
	For a Brush		1	1
	For a Broom			3
	For fees etc. at the Visitation	1	17	6
	For a Curate's Licence		10	0
	The Glazier's Bill		3	8
	For Parchment		1	6
	For new Posts & Bars to the Churchyard	3	13	0
	For Paint and oil to the Churchyard			
	Posts and Bars	8	15	10
		19	5	9
	In hand		1	1½
		19	4	7½
	Sum collected	19	4	1½
	Due to the Churchwardens			6

This money, of course, was spent only on the upkeep of the church and does not take into consideration the many disbursements made in the form of alms for the poor.

Alton St Pancras is a small village of some 120 souls, but in the past it was large enough to accommodate three great houses: Alton Australis, south-east of the church where the Manor is to-day; Alton Borealis, north of the church, presumably on the site of Austral Farm; and Alton Pancras, further north still and believed to be equivalent to the modern Barcombe Grange. All three houses stood on the west side of the stream which, with the common highway, divided Barcombe Grange from its garden on the east bank. In the 1860s Barcombe Grange was demolished and a new house built on the east bank, but the walls of the Tudor enclosed garden remain to this day.

At first glance there is nothing exceptional about Alton St Pancras: no shop, no public house, no school, no children's playground, no village hall. But these are minor inconveniences. It is a lovely place, with a gentle, unspectacular beauty that far transcends obvious prettiness. Every house in the village enjoys views over green fields and country, and to leave the road and wander over the quiet, peaceful hills is to enter into the very heart of England.

THE BALLAD OF ST PANCRAS

Pancras was born in Phrygia,
An orphan boy was he;
His uncle he had charge of him
And took him to a far country.

In Rome they heard the name of Christ
And followed in his ways,
But persecution was their lot
And martyrdom their case.

To die for faith when but a lad
Earned Pancras a saint's crown,
His name spread down the centuries
Till it reached an English town.

Augustine, to save Saxon souls
To Canterbury came,
The first church that he founded there
Honoured St Pancras' name.

The Saxons wanted Pancras' bones
A relic for to be;
King Oswill of Northumbria
Was sent them from Rome's see.

A village down in Wessex
At the source of the Piddle stream
Took its name and its church from St Pancras,
Held in high esteem.

Now honour we St Pancras
With all our might and main,
Source of our homes, source of our faith,
Whose light will never wane.

ANON.

Plush

THE VILLAGE AND THE CHURCH

Known in ancient records variously as Plais, P'lis, Perlis,
Plisshe and Plus, the Plush of today is a deep valley running
from south-west to north-east, surrounded by a horseshoe
of hills all of which contain remains of previous settlements
of the Roman, Bronze and Iron Ages as well as some which
may be even earlier. On West Hill, Celtic field systems can
be seen in many places where they have not been destroyed
by modern ploughing. Between Ball Hill and Church Hill
there are squares and ramparts and a well-preserved
symmetrical barrow on the way to Alton St Pancras. Fur-
·ther eastward on Nettlecombe Tout dykes and ditches are
still visible to this day.

Various theories have been advanced about Nettlecombe
Tout. Its unique position at the head of the valley, and its
height giving views to Glastonbury Tor and over Blackmore Vale, make it a naturally secure fortress, except on the
south-east side where the dykes have been made. Charles
Warne, in *Ancient Dorset*, suggests that it was a retreat: '*tout*'
meaning refuge. On the other hand, '*toute*' or '*teute*' might
refer to a Celtic god, and the hill could have been a place
sacred for worship and sacrifice. There is also the legend of a
trial of strength between two giants on the Tout to see who
could throw a stone the greater distance. The loser is said to
be buried by the two huge boulders which stand on a place
known as The Giant's Grave beneath the hill.

Plush Brook rises near the site of a twelfth-century chapel
of ease dedicated to St John the Baptist. The little steam
flows along the valley until it joins the River Piddle near
Piddletrenthide Manor House. Although it contains very
little water during much of the year, the Brook has been

known to rise quickly to two or three feet after severe rainstorms and inundate the surrounding cottages. One of the worst floods in living memory occurred at the end of May 1979, when many of the ground floors of the cottages were flooded and left with a thick layer of evil-smelling silt when the water subsided.

Until 1847, when the present chapel was built, there was no burial ground for the people of Plush. Corpses had to be carried by horse and cart from the village along Plush Brook and then up past the old chapel by Rockpits Farm over the hills to Buckland Newton, a distance of about three miles. The ancient track still exists, and it is said that the rumbling of ghostly carts can still be heard on their way to Buckland Newton Church, where there is a special door through which the coffins were carried. The hills are steep and windswept, and not long ago a man lost his way in the snow and froze to death as he tried to reach Buckland.

Plush was in the parish of Buckland Newton from the twelfth century until 1936, when it was joined to the neighbouring parish of Mappowder. Later it became a part of Piddletrenthide and remains so. In the early days, Buckland belonged to Glastonbury Abbey, and Plush, as a manor on its own, was also owned by the Abbey. A manorial survey of 1327 gives a picture of farming life in the village at that time, setting out the names of the Abbey tenants and the rents and obligations due from them. One Alfredus de Plis, for instance, held four acres and paid a two-shilling rent. It was his duty to

shear the sheep and mow the meadow of the lord and work from the second day after the Feast of St John the Baptist [24 June] until Chains [1 August] and all day after that until the Feast of St Michael and All Angels [29 September]. He ought to thresh and reap weekly one load of wheat or two of barley or oats. And he has a small linen cloth full of straw and gives four hens as churchscot in addition to three hens because his cows do not lie in the lord's fold. When he reaps an acre he has two corigia [a binding thong] sheares. He receives from the lord on Christmas day a meal for himself and his wife and two loaves, three dishes. For his servant one loaf, meat and venison and husbote and haybote and fuel for Christmas.

Soon after the date of this Manorial Survey came the disaster of the Black Death in the years 1348 and 1349. It was brought in by the crew of a ship which landed at Weymouth, and Dorset was very badly hit. Thirty years after this catastrophe, Wat Tyler led the Peasants' Revolt and life in village communities began to change. It was the beginning of the rise of the yeoman farmer and in 1497 there is mentioned for the first time a member of the Miller family, later to own the whole of Plush estate. The record is an interesting one, for it chronicles the fact that on that date Robert Miller of Plush was fined twenty shillings for giving food to fugitives fleeing from the abortive Perkin Warbeck Rebellion against King Henry VII.

There is no mention of the little Chapel of Ease tucked into the fold of the hills near Rockpits Farm until the year 1573, when Queen Elizabeth I wrote a letter asking many questions concerning 'the image of Our Lady in the Chapple of Plush, worshipped with offrynges of the people and any brotherhood of Our Lady belonginge to the same chappell.' No doubt such idolatry smacked of the catholicism which still threatened the stability of the throne and the Queen demanded an explanation. The questions were put to the inhabitants of the village but only one old man, aged ninety – a remarkable age for those days – was apparently able to reply and it is recorded that he said:

. . . that he hath knowen that dyvers women have come to the image of Our Lady in the Chappell of Plushe aforesaide and have offered unt' the same image certayn candells of wax and other worshipping of the same image this deponent knoweth not.

This deponent sayeth he did not knowe any brotherhood of Our Lady belonging to the same chappell of Plushe but he sayeth that those that dwelt within the same village of Plusche did yerely keep a helpe ale to mayntayne the same chapple but how many shepe or kyne there dyd belong to the same chappell this deponent knoweth not but he sayeth that there were both shepe and kyne belonging to the same and that some of them were yerely kylled for the helpe ale.

The deponant had never known of the offering of any gold rings, but he sayeth that he hath knowne dyvers sylver ringes to be given by women to the maytenance of the said chappell when they lay at the point of death and that this deponent when he was warden of the same chappell did receive fower ringes which he delyv'd on to the next warden that followed him. Further that he dyd never knowe any ringes hanged upon any festyval days about the neck of the said Image nor at any other tyme.

That when the help ale was he that was appointed warden or steward would make his accompte of such things as was given to make the same church ale and what remayned of the on' plus [?] was always restored upin the reparacons of the same.

A 'help ale' was a festival, part religious and part secular, during which ale was brewed in the churchyard and sometimes inside the church. Nothing is known of the outcome of the Queen's investigation or what happened to the statue of Our Lady in the chapel. Perhaps it was removed on direct orders from Elizabeth herself.

In 1650 Plush petitioned unsuccessfully to be made a parish on its own. This largely arose because at that time it was in the cure of a man named Guillaume who was accused of leading a very disorderly and debauched life and of having 'for wages £14 per year and other unlawful earnings.' It is said that the parishioners showed their dislike of him by putting a broody hen with her chicks in the pulpit before he preached. Later, within living memory, a similar event occurred when the parson taking a service in Plush church started his sermon by saying: 'Would ye please remove this bag of ferrets before I begin my sermon!'

From the end of the fifteenth century until the year 1880, the name of Miller was prominent in the history of Plush and its farms. For these 400 years it is the saga of a family who became more and more prosperous until in the end there was a financial collapse and the entire estate had to be sold. Although records are few and far between, the will of a certain Roger Miller, dated 1596, shows the nature both of his position and his possessions:

> I bequeath my body to be buried in Buckland Newton.
> I give to all my brothers and sister 13/4 a-piece
> To my four godchildren 4 cheap [sheep]
> To Edward Rose of Seazon [Cerne] 10/-

To my 3 servants dwelling with me 3/-

To my daughter in law Mathew Channell £5

To my son in law Giles Claville £5 if he be living

To my son in law Robert Clavyle 1 cow

To my brother Edward my best gold ring

To my brother Michael my 2nd gold ring

To Grace Howse my 3rd gold ring

To Elizabeth Howse my 4th and worst gold ring

To Robert and Mary Marche 1 ewe and 1 lamb a-piece

To Christopher Hayne ½ a bushel of barley

To John Stride my Father in law 13/4

To the poor of Plushe and of the Tithing of Knoll 3/4 severally

To my brother Edward Miller and my cousin Roger Howse shall have £60 delivered to them in discharge of the bond they have given with me to William Roberts

All the rest of my goods unbequeathed I give to my wife whom I make my executrix and John Barleycorne, Michael Miller and Robert Howse my overseers.

Proved 24 November 1597

During the seventeenth, eighteenth and nineteenth centuries the Millers flourished, acquiring more and more land, including the Manor House, Harveys Farm House, the Knap (now the Brace of Pheasants public house) and other lands and cottages. In 1848 the little church was built, not on the site of the chapel of ease, which was considered too far from the centre of the village, but on a knoll behind the Manor House and on the road to Mappowder. Dedicated, like the ancient chapel, to St John the Baptist, the church, which was renovated in 1883, has attractive stained glass and no tower but a small turret to house the two bells. There is an interesting little anecdote concerning these bells. For some time they had not been used and then, last year, one of the churchwardens, sweeping up a litter of dead bees that had nested in the roof, noticed that the bells were not in their usual place. The police were notified, and they reported that two bells had been found in a field in the village of Martinstown, several miles away. Presumably the thieves had decided that their booty could not be disposed of and must be dumped.

In 1880, as has already been said, the Miller family were obliged to sell the estate to pay their debts. For a time it became a shooting reserve, with the Manor a lodge. Again bankruptcy forced a sale, and in the year 1899 the Manor and lands were bought by the Mayor of Weymouth for the sum of £8300. After this change of ownership, the history of Plush is somewhat sketchily documented until the Second World War, when the then owner, a Mr Graham, also became bankrupt – a fate which seems to have befallen the majority of the estate owners! – and sold Plush to Mr Barnard Hankey.

When the new owner took over the village he found it in a sorry state. Many of the nineteen cottages were decayed and derelict, with gaping thatch and broken windows. There was no electricity. Water for all purposes had to be drawn from wells or from one communal village pump. The school, where one elderly spinster taught children of all ages in one small room, had been closed for fifteen years. There was no post office, no shop, no public house, no telephone. The nearest public transport was two miles away in Piddletrenthide.

But John Hankey was not dismayed. He was determined to transform Plush into a model village, and within a very few years electricity and running water had been laid on, the pair of cottages known as the Knap had become a public house, the Hankey Arms, and every single cottage had been rebuilt or renovated, provided with a bathroom and given new thatch and whitewashed walls. One cottage was converted into a village shop. And if the farm workers were to be made more comfortable and so persuaded to stay in the village, so were the farm animals: in a short time a new set of buildings had been erected in place of the derelict byres, capable of accommodating 100 cows to be milked by machinery.

In this way Plush was re-born.

For ten years the resurrected village prospered and with it the squire, who divided his time between two diverse interests: the Plush herd of Red Poll cattle, which earned him an international reputation, and the cultivation of beautiful and exotic orchids. But in the end, following the sad example of his predecessors, he found the estate too great a financial burden and was obliged to put the whole village up for auction. Although opening bids of £100,000 were invited, no offers were received and the estate was finally sold in separate lots, some to sitting tenants who continue to live and farm in Plush.

There is still no school and no longer a shop, although the inn, now known as the Brace of Pheasants, remains, rebuilt after being destroyed by fire last year. Public transport takes villagers to Dorchester twice a week. New houses appear from time to time and are integrated into the community. But even today, in 1980, Plush is a hamlet which time seems to have passed by. The stranger, approaching it along the road that leads from the Valley and winds among the folded hills, is aware of an enclosed, dream-like atmosphere, a feeling of remoteness and seclusion, as though the village hugs to itself a secret which only those that live there can truly understand.

THE ORCHID NURSERY

Tucked away behind the Brace of Pheasants are seven glass houses which go to make up one of the most unusual and exotic projects to be found in the heart of the Dorset countryside. Many call it an orchid farm, but the owner, Mr Keith Andrew, prefers to call it an orchid nursery. Although he does a lot of business in cut flowers and orchids as pot plants, Mr Andrew's real interest is in breeding.

'To put it in horsey terms,' he says, 'you could call us a stud farm, providing the breeding stock from which hybrids are sent all over the world.'

Orchids grow in every continent apart from the polar regions, although they are most abundant and most varied in the temperate regions of the Andes of Colombia and in Sikkim. In England there are nearly forty species growing wild, including the bee orchid and the twayblade, which can be found growing on the chalk hillsides of Plush itself.

Some people look upon orchids as the most beautiful flowers in the whole botanic kingdom; to others they seem bizarre creations from distant lands, half animal and half plant, in some way like visitors from outer space. Perhaps it is the way in which the flower perches on its stem like a bee or a butterfly poised for instant flight; or the intricate shape of the curved petals; or the spots and splashes of brilliant colour that seem to hold a weird, esoteric significance. Maybe it is the strangeness of the epiphytic species which grow on rocks and on the branches of trees, seeming to draw their sustenance from the air. However they are regarded, they are certainly not what you would expect to find in a village that depends on homely agriculture for its existence.

The Plush nursery has developed from a private collection once owned by Mr Barnard Hankey, who bought the village of Plush in the 1940s and commercialized his hobby by turning it into Dorset Orchids. Six years later Keith Andrew joined the company and in 1966 took it over himself.

Since then the business has flourished. The whole purpose is to produce new breeding lines and to improve the quality of the existing ones. It is necessary to win awards and certificates from the Royal Horticultural Society for the new strains; without them it is difficult to sell to other breeders and hybridizers, and so quality is all-important.

About thirty to forty crosses take place in one year, each producing some 25,000 seedlings. The delicate operation, done of course in the wild by insects, is achieved by Mr Andrew with the help of a matchstick. One of the most important things is to ensure that no stray insect makes its way into the nursery. Says Mr Andrew, 'A bee or even a large fly can ruin our entire crop by cross-pollinating plants we don't want fertilized.'

Once cross-pollination has been effected, a long period of patient waiting follows, for the development of a new hybrid can take between four and eight years. Even after that time there is no guarantee that the orchid which eventually opens will be worth all the time and trouble.

'It is a long process,' admits Mr Andrew, 'and we have to

wait a long time to see if our guesses and intuitions are correct, but it's usually worth it to see a new orchid.'

After being pollinated, the orchid produces a seed pod containing up to half a million seeds. When that has matured, a process which can take up to a year, the seeds are removed to a laboratory and put on a special culture in sterile conditions and under artificial light. There they are left to germinate. There is always excitement when germination takes place, for the long-drawn-out process is at last under way. The tiny seedlings are transferred to another culture and grown on until they reach a height of about five inches. Then they are pricked out in pulverized fir bark to grow into mature plants. Watering and feeding is carried on by the patient orchidist until, years later, the long-awaited flower opens, and perhaps a new and exquisite orchid has been born.

Country Crafts and Pursuits

YESTERDAY'S SHEEP

Until very recently the Piddle Valley was a valley of sheep. From either side of the valley road rose fields thick with contented ewes and their frisking lambs. The names of the fields themselves sound like a Dorset incantation and in many cases recall the names of former owners: Putt Ground, Wallace's, Beck's Bottom and Bats; Mitchells, Smart's Ground, the Big Down and Twenty-Acre; Young's Corner, Horse Ground, Pitman's and Racklands; Dutnol, Ewe Leaze, Hog Leaze and Highlands; the Friaries, Gert Ground, Roger's Bottom and King Grove. I worked for David Wightman – and still do, although no longer with sheep – and to my mind there is no country sight more beautiful than a field studded with a flock of Dorset Horns. Sadly it is a sight that I shall almost certainly never see again.

As early as the 1930s the sheep began to go, when Charlie Smart persuaded his father, who had started farming with two acres and finished up with 2000, that there was more money in cattle than in sheep. At Piddlehinton, Bill Lovelace still farms Dorset Downs and his father, Rex, won many prizes for them at agricultural shows, but our Dorset Horns are gone for ever. Dorset Horns were kept because they drop October lambs which are fat in time for the Spring and Easter market. It is traditional for people to eat lamb for their Easter Sunday dinner, symbolic of the Paschal Lamb slain and eaten at the Feast of the Passover and also of the Resurrection of the Lamb of God, and so there was always a ready market.

Our shepherd's year began in May, when the old ewes –

six-tooth, as they are called, from the number of incisors in the top jaw – were drafted out of the flock and sent to the May Fair in Dorchester. Before going they would be 'tailed', or 'crutched', as some shepherds say: a quick clip under the tail to clear away the caked dung and winter mud and so facilitate a cleaner fleece for shearing. Nowadays the sheep are taken to the Fair in lorries, but then we drove them on foot, the old ewes and any surplus hogs, along the Valley, up over Piddlehinton Hill and across to Charminster, where they spent the night in Harold Miles's field. The next morning we would be back in Charminster at five, three of us and perhaps a couple of dogs, to drive them on to Dorchester, where we would arrive at eight o'clock. Sometimes we would meet more flocks being driven along the road from other directions. In good weather it was a lovely journey in the breaking dawn, but sometimes it poured with rain and by the time we reached Dorchester we would be soaked to the skin and the sheep sodden.

The market was a mosaic of noise and colour and movement: the ewes blaring, the lambs bleating and the shepherds shouting as they found the pens allotted to them, pulled out the sheep from their flock and divided them by age and quality into separate lots of ten, twenty or thirty sheep. By this method of selling the five-year-old ewes, approximately one-third of the flock was changed each year and it was kept young and vigorous. We usually had five rams to serve the ewes – one ram to fifty ewes – and sometimes we would buy a ram at the Fair to renew our stock.

Directly after the May Fair the rest of the flock were washed in a deep pool of running water cut out of the River Piddle behind South House. The Wash Pool was about ten feet across and four to five feet deep. The sheep were first hurdled up and then thrown in one at a time while men with poles known as 'rubbers' stood ready to push their heads under the water and make sure that they were totally immersed. It was a wonderful sight. The sheep would swim about for a minute or two and then walk up a ramp at the other end and drain off. The object of the washing was to clean the fleece – you can get a better price for washed wool

– but also to bring the grease out of the fleece and so make the shearing easier. An unwashed fleece clogs the clippers with solid grease and makes the work much more arduous. Four or five days after the wash we would start shearing. Shearing is the hardest manual job in the whole of farming and the most skilful. It has been described by New Zealander Godfrey Bowen, perhaps the greatest exponent of the art, as work that calls for 'much more than just physical strength and exuberance – rather for balance, grace, rhythm, suppleness, with eye, brain and hand in smart co-ordination.' It is a perfectionist job: if you don't hold your hand exactly right you 'bootlace' the sheep – take off a slice of the flesh. If there is a wrinkle of skin you can easily cut off the wrinkle. Particular care has to be taken not to cut off the ewe's teats: this has happened to inexperienced shearers the world over! If a second wrong cut is made the wool is spoiled and can be sold only as 'sweepings'. In the hands of an expert the work looks easy, but if you have never sheared before you can spend at least an hour with one sheep and you cannot claim to be a real expert until you have sheared a thousand.

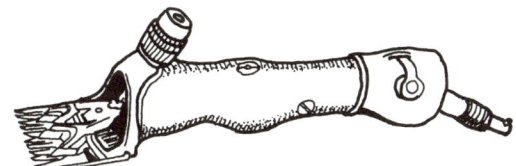

I used to set up a particular shearing system for David Wightman at the drier where the sheep were penned overnight so that the fleeces were dry and an early start could be made the following morning. They were penned in two catching pens immediately behind the shear board, and the shepherd would keep them pushed up behind the shearers and release them one at a time through the gate. Our shepherd – Fred Vatcher was his name although he was never known as anything but Shep – and Charlie Legg would ensure that there was a continuous supply of sheep in the catching pens while Brian Dibben and I got on with the shearing.

There is a marvellous ritual about the process, the 'blows', as the cutting strokes are called, being precise movements always starting at the same place and carrying on until the fleece falls away in one piece. If you do not do it exactly – off the brisket, across the belly and round the crutch and so on – the wool gets in the way of the next 'blow' and will not fall off correctly. A good man can shear a sheep in one minute – although not in the case of Dorset Horns as they are big sheep and shearing round the horns takes more time. I used to manage sixty-three a day and Brian Dibben could complete more than a hundred. Although the work is painfully hard and brings total exhaustion at the end of the day, it is a kind of drug that gets hold of you and has a strange thrill and beauty of its own.

In the old days, some fifty years ago, gangs of men used to go round the farms at shearing time to offer their services. The work went on for days, and at night they would sleep on the fleeces until dawn broke and they could resume work. Hand shears were used then. The days of the hand shearers, or 'blade men' as they were known, were followed by the use of mechanical clippers. My own introduction to shearing started with an old Lister petrol engine with belt drive and cable attached to the clippers, and it would go putt-putting away throughout the day. As we carried on with the work the sheared fleeces would be tied up and stacked high, and during our meal break Brian Dibben and I would lean back on the stack of fleeces, the warmest and softest couch imaginable. Many flocks are now sheared by contractors, and men who have acquired the necessary skill can be well rewarded for their efforts.

After they are sheared, the sheep are stamped with an identification mark – in our case 'W' for Wightman – two-tooth ewes on the shoulder, four-tooth ewes in their second breeding year on the middle back, and six-tooth ewes on the rump. In this way it is easy later on to pick out those due to be drafted out of the flock. Although the marks are stamped on directly after shearing, they come up with the wool and can still be seen when the fleece is grown.

It is now that the rams are sent in, raddled with a manufactured dye (a far cry from the days of Thomas Hardy's

Riddleman in *The Return of the Native*), so that the shepherd can see at a glance which ewes have been served. The gestation period is five months, and so the lambs are ready to be born in October. All the ewes are dipped in July to get rid of ticks, and then they are put out together in the fields, cropping the summer grass until the time for birth draws near. At this time the hurdle-flock system of enclosures is used, whereby the ewes are given a new section of field to crop each day. Hurdles of hazel stems have largely been replaced by the less picturesque wire fences. The erection of the hurdles is known as 'pitching out', and by this means the shepherd can keep an eye on his flock and see at once which ewes have given birth.

Female lambs are known as 'chilvers' and male lambs as 'wethers'. All are docked soon after they are born and the wethers are castrated. The old harvest fields of cereal have been undersown with grass, and this enables the ewes with their lambs to thrive and grow undisturbed in the early stages. When darkness falls we go out for 'coupling up', to make sure that the lambs are back with their mothers for the night. The ewes blare to bring their lambs back to their sides. Sometimes a stray will bleat pitifully, unable to find its dam, but experienced shepherds seem to know by instinct which lamb belongs to which ewe, and even in a flock of 300 or 400 they have an uncanny knack of being able to identify mother and child.

In November, when the grass is finished, the sheep are put on roots, kale and swede grown specially for the purpose, and are folded again. Years ago someone would be sent round with a swede-hacker to dig up the roots (Hardy's Tess eked out a scanty existence in this way at Flintcomb-Ash) but the need for economy has put an end to this. 'Creeps' are constructed within the folds with rails so close that only the lambs can creep through to eat the cream of the kale and cake for fattening, the ewes being made to wait their turn outside.

By Easter all the wethers have grown fat and have been sent to market. The female lambs remain chilvers for the rest of their first year, get sheared at six months with the rest of the flock and then at eighteen months are known as hogs.

In that May they go to the rams, have a crop of lambs for the next three years and are then drafted out to market at the age of five, and so the whole cycle begins again.

All the wool would eventually arrive at the Yorkshire woollen mills to be made almost invariably into garments, as both Dorset Horns and Dorset Downs provide a very high-quality wool. The lamb meat was sent everywhere: one year it was reputed to be in great demand for Grace Kelly's wedding banquet! But all that is past history. The end came about four years ago, not with the eight-mile walk to market of earlier years but in Tallons Lane with the loading of the entire flock into cattle lorries for their journey to the May Fair. Bill Lovelace still farms his Dorset Downs in Piddlehinton, but Piddletrenthide's Dorset Horns are gone for good.

GEORGE JAKEMAN

. . . AND TODAY'S CATTLE

Thus fundamental and far-reaching changes came to the Piddle Valley. After hundreds of years, ever-tighter margins decreed that the sheep must go and milk production take their place. 'Charles was right,' said William Smart, who farmed with his son on the west side of the Valley. His son had advocated the change. William was reluctant to say goodbye to the sheep but later agreed that his son had made the right decision.

To obtain the required stock it was decided to buy Irish cattle with a preponderance of roan shorthorns. A dealer in the Blackmore Vale was the main supplier. We would walk into his fields, look at a bunch of down-calving heifers and select, by eye alone, those which we considered had the greatest milk potential. Offers from the farmer and counter-offers from the dealer went to and fro for some time until eventually a handshake sealed the bargain.

Dairy farming in this area was carried on with bought-in cattle, known in agricultural circles as a 'flying herd', when milk yields per cow were in the region of 650 to 700 gallons per lactation. This lactation period represents 305 days in the year. The remaining sixty days are the drying-off period, hence the need to calve a cow every twelve months to maintain the yield. Since the introduction of artificial insemination milking herds have become self-sufficient, with a dramatic increase in yield. Dairies with a herd average of over 1000 gallons per year are common, and this can undoubtedly be attributed to better breeding and an increased awareness of feed requirements.

In the forties the hand milking of cows began to decline. The task, always an onerous one, has become only a memory of those occasional disasters when bucket, stool and milker would part company and the floor of the milking shed would be white with spilt milk. Composure and equilibrium had to be restored before 'Buttercup's' confidence could once again be obtained. You certainly needed to be a saint when milking cows!

Gradually we have said goodbye to the blue and red roan shorthorns, which served the area so well; by now genes from the Friesian bulls have created a black and white scene throughout the Valley. The value of the Friesian lies in the dual role of the breed: the potential to produce milk and then at the end of the cow's milking life to provide a carcase well covered with beef for the butcher. Canadian Holstein cattle are black and white animals virtually identical with Friesians, but although they have high milk yield potential, astute calf buyers pass them over because they do not possess the same muscling capability on the hind quarters.

The trend in agriculture towards a reduced labour force is seen most clearly in livestock units. Whereas in the past eight hand milkers would have been required for a herd of 120 cows, this task is now performed by one man, a reduction made possible by the mechanical advancement in milking equipment and the milking techniques which have evolved. In the 'good old days' it was said that the farmer would plan the day's work while sitting on a stool under a cow as he helped with the early morning milking. Today the Land Rover is a substitute for the milking-stool as a place for planning the work routine!

For an effective milk yield a cow must produce a calf every year. To ensure this, not only must there be close liaison with the veterinary surgeon but also all the staff on a mixed farm must be able successfully to apply their stock-manship, their ability to observe any abnormality in the animals. The detection of the heat period in a cow is not always easy, and no livestock can thrive consistently without constant vigilance.

Every year a new batch of heifers is introduced into the dairy unit. This has a twofold purpose: to replace the older cows that are being culled at the end of their working life and to maintain the quality of the milk produced with higher solids and butterfat. Of all the calves born, the females are retained for a future place in the dairy herd while the bull calves are weaned from their dams until Christmas, when they are reared for 'eighteen-month beef '. The first calving heifers run with a beef-type bull because it is finer boned, and this makes for easier calving; also when cattle are outlying the use of artificial insemination is virtually impossible.

It is very gratifying for the stockman when his animals give birth to their young satisfactorily. Conversely, a loss at birth can make him very despondent. Animals endure their discomfort stoically and a good stockman is always on the alert to note when the udder is well stocked and exuding milk, when the vulva pinks up and when, in Dorset par-lance, the cow 'pitches in' and finally creeps off on her own. Finally the calf arrives or, if it does not appear within an hour of 'bladdering' (the Dorset stockman's term for the expulsion of the outer membranes or water-bag), the cow must be examined to make sure that presentation is normal and that no help is required. To thrive, a calf must obtain the colostrum milk from its mother – the cow's first milk after giving birth – and yet in the first few hours of its life it finds progress a struggle; it is therefore essential to make sure that it suckles as soon as possible. After producing their fourth calf, cows are liable to suffer from milk fever, caused by a drop in the calcium content of the circulating blood, and when they succumb immediate calcium replacement is essential. The animal often becomes comatose and you have to insert a needle into the jugular vein to feed the calcium into the bloodstream. To watch the cow's nose break into liquid droplets and the ears start to flick, to see an awareness in the eye that life is surging back, is to me the most exhilarating experience in the handling of livestock.

Another serious cattle problem is the incidence of bloat caused by fermenting gases in the rumen – the paunch or first stomach of a cow. The distension usually caused by lush pasture can very quickly asphyxiate an animal unless quick action is taken, and although farms usually carry a stock of bloat drenches these are effective only if the stockman has enough time to use them. A trocar and cannula are the correct instruments for the job, but most stockmen are compelled to use a knife, making a deep incision in the side which gives immediate respiratory relief to the affected animal. In spite of the gravity of such conditions, I can recall some amusing incidents. On one occasion David Wightman and I realized that something was not quite right in a field known as Beck's Bottom. All the cattle were milling around in a circle and when we investigated we found that one of the animals was 'blown' and needed immediate attention. The only tool available was the ever-faithful knife and using it saved the cow, but in the excitement we did not notice that the young lad accompanying us had vanished. We then saw that all the other animals had moved away from the scene of the drama and grouped themselves thirty yards away. A closer look revealed that Dan, unable to stomach the surgery, had walked away and promptly fainted, to become the centre of bovine attention and curiosity.

There are three farms in the Valley engaged on milk production, but in recent years there has been a new development, the production of beef under the system known as 'single suckling'. This allows the calf to remain with its dam until it is weaned in preparation for the birth of the next calf. After weaning, the calves go into the cattle yards for final fattening. The uproar when they are weaned from their mothers is an experience shared by the whole Valley: the animals blare incessantly for two days until the anguish subsides. Nevertheless perhaps their lot is better than that of the milking cow who is separated from her calf four days after the birth.

GEORGE JAKEMAN

Edgar Tory, of Higher Waterston Farm, tells of the time, before the use of combine harvesters, when he would spend days and days with his men threshing the corn. The bottom of the rick, when they reached it, was always thick with mouse nests, filled with pink, hairless newborn mice. 'There was one chap,' remembers Mr Tory, 'and I can't recall his name, who used to pick up the tiny naked mice and swallow them whole, like oysters!'

Mrs Cristabel Green of Piddlehinton remembers how, seventy years ago, she and her five sisters – the Chaldecott girls – used to be sent out to play in the field known as Mill Ground where the chickens were kept, and how they were told to sit in a circle round the grass in order to keep the foxes away.

She also recalls the time when her grandmother lived in White Lackington in a house without a well and it was the girls' task to carry water up to her from their home at Fleet House each day.

THE PIGS OF PIDDLEHINTON

Fifty years ago or more there were no large herds of pigs in the Piddle Valley. Many of the villagers kept a pig of their own, or perhaps a couple, which were fed on garden waste and household scraps. Farmers with dairy herds may have had herds of pigs, but they were small by today's standards. At this time there was comparatively little transport, and so the milk produced in the Valley could not easily be taken out. Accordingly, when there was a flush of milk in the spring and early summer, the surplus was made into cheese and butter: this was a means of storing the excess milk for future use. The whey left from the cheese-making and the buttermilk from the butter-making, together with local-grown barley, were fed to the pigs.

In the autumn, when the cows were beginning to go dry and there was no surplus milk and therefore no cheese-making and no whey, the pigs were sold to the local butcher to be slaughtered, salted and smoked and the 'stored surplus of milk' became a food to be eaten during the lean winter months. The pig kept by the cottager was slaughtered as a source of meat for him and his family.

Slaughtering for home consumption was not the humane business it is in the abattoir of today. The pig would be dragged up to a bundle of wheat straw, its throat would be cut and it would be held down by a couple of men until it bled to death. The straw would be laid over the carcase and lit, to singe the skin, and the straw and ashes would then be washed off and the singed skin scraped.

The pig would then be 'hardled'. (The process is known as 'hardling' in Dorset, 'legging' in Kent and 'hamstringing' in Essex.) A piece of notched wood, with a rope tied to it, would be threaded through the hamstrings, and the carcase hung up on staples in the beams of the back kitchen to be gutted and cleaned. After a couple of days, when the meat was 'set', the carcase would be cut into joints, some to be cooked and eaten as pork, the rest to be salted or perhaps smoked to provide bacon and ham. The head, trotters and other odd bits of meat were usually made into brawn. In those days the pigs carried much more fat than our modern breeds, and this was rendered down into lard and used for cooking and pastry-making.

The bacon and ham in those days were cured by rubbing salt into the meat and then letting it lie in a lead trough or 'silt' for several weeks. It was then packed in linen bags and stored in a rack hanging from the kitchen ceiling. The meat was very salty to eat and became extremely rank, and if kept until the following summer attracted the flies. An old acquaintance of mine told me of the time when, as a boy, he was sitting in the kitchen having a meal with his parents, his brothers and sisters, when a maggot fell from a racked ham on to the table.

'See that?' remarked his father. "Bout time we got thik 'am down and ate 'e!'

Nothing of the pig would be wasted. Even the intestines would be made into 'chitlings'. To clean them, they were turned inside out. Tradition said that they had to be turned three times before they were fit to eat. When Tom Wightman kept the butcher's shop in Piddletrenthide and killed pigs, he used to take the chitlings down to the Piddle and let the river run through them to clean them. Another method was to put them on a tap, turn on the water and wash them right out. When they were clean, you would plait them up and fry them like black puddings.

Today, the cycle continues with even more inter-dependence between pig farm and dairy farm. The dung produced by our pigs at Bourne Farm we put on the grass as fertilizer. The grass is dried and made into cubes which are sold to the dairy farmer. The farmer's cows eat the dried grass cubes and their milk is taken to factories where it is made into butter and cheese; these, in turn, produce skim milk and whey which is fed to the pigs.

Because of modern methods of transport, deep freezes and different methods of producing meat, the cycle goes on nowadays all the year round. Indeed, if it were not for our pigs a different use would have to be found for the whey. It cannot be put down the drain and into the sewage works because of the high acidity. In fact, last year when there was a surplus of whey it had to be taken to Bridport and pumped out to sea.

At Bourne Farm we used 12,000 gallons of whey and buttermilk each day. If for any reason the road tankers cannot bring it out to us, there would not be room in the storage tanks at the dairy for the next lot of milk. So we are as vital to the dairies and to the cheese and butter manufacturers as they are to us.

Our company started farming pigs at Hanford Farm by buying up store pigs between twelve and fourteen weeks old, weighing 60 to 70 pounds, and fattening them on until they weighed 260 to 270 pounds. The disadvantage of this system was that every time we brought in a fresh batch of pigs we brought with them a fresh set of diseases, and the whole thing became a risky business. So we decided to become breeders ourselves to have some control over the type of pig we were producing. We bought Bourne Farm and 200 gilts (young sows) to start us off.

We began with the extensive system: we used to run the pigs out in large pens with temporary portable huts which we moved around the farm, putting them in different fields each year. However, we found that this system was not an economic one. It used a lot of labour; it was very difficult in continual wet and cold weather, with heavy losses of small pigs due to chilling; and when the sows farrowed foxes would often take the piglets. No fence could keep them away. Edgar Tory has told me that when myxomatosis was at its height and rabbits were scarce, he found the outside of a fox's earth in Doles Wood scattered not only with the remains of moles, rats, rooks and mice but also with the little legs and trotters of piglets that the vixen had brought home to her litter of cubs.

The intensive system was thus more or less forced upon us. In any case, increasing numbers of pigs had already almost turned our extensive system into an intensive one and finally we decided to go fully intensive with all the pigs indoors.

As I have already implied, the chief risk in pig breeding is disease. At Bourne, everyone who visits the pigs or works with them has to leave his clothing outside, take a shower and change into clean clothes before going in. Washing the hair is most important of all, for hair can harbour viruses for several hours. For instance, should you happen to be walking in Dorchester when a load of pigs went past, and should some of those pigs have pneumonia or any other virus, if the smell of the pigs reached you the virus could also reach you and lodge in your hair. If you then went on to Bourne Farm and the virus was transferred to one single pig, the disease could spread to the whole herd and never be eradicated. So the rule remains: anyone going off the farm has to take a shower when next he comes in. What is more, the rule seems to work; we no longer have the disease problems we used to get. Needless to say, the diseases involved are peculiar to pigs and have no effect on humans, horses, cattle or domestic animals.

Today at Bourne we have 1000 sows and their progeny, 12,000 pigs altogether. The pigs are sold when they are six months old and weigh 220 pounds although occasionally we fatten them on to 270 pounds. They are sent live to Bowyer's factory at Trowbridge in Wiltshire, where they are slaughtered and used for various purposes: pork pies, sausages, pre-packed bacon, ham and so on. The sows produce six litters in their lifetime – 2·3 litters a year – and are then replaced. The gestation period is four months. After farrowing, the sow suckles her piglets for three weeks, has a rest period of seven to ten days, and then goes back to the boar; so this rest period is the only time when she is doing nothing, neither gestating nor lactating.

Everything on the farm is highly mechanized. We cut the grass, which has been grown with the benefit of the pig slurry as fertilizer, up to six times a year and the dried grass cubes are the most efficient method of conservation possible. All you do is take the moisture out, leaving ninety-eight percent of the original feed value of the grass in the cube. Much of the feed value of grass grown with artificial fertilizers derived from oil is wasted when made into silage or hay. Silage-making gives seventy-five percent of the original feed value if you are lucky, hay-making fifty percent. So although a lot of oil is used in our grass drier, the method is much the most efficient, particularly as we have used natural fertilizer in place of oil-based chemical fertilizer.

Pig keeping, like farming generally, has changed enormously over the years. Nowadays everything has to be done intensively. The methods used may not always be to the liking of the farmer, but in the end they are forced upon him by economic circumstances and by the public demand for cheap food.

ALAN READ

MASTER THATCHER

I started work on a farm when I was twelve years old. The hours were from six in the morning until six in the evening, Saturdays and Sundays included, and the pay was six old pence (2½p) a day. Later I had a job in some gravel pits, cycling to Bere Regis and a mile beyond, digging out gravel. This time I left home at five a.m. and got home at nine o'clock at night. Then, when I was twenty-six, I saw an advertisement in the paper for a thatching job. I tried for it and got it. I was the last man to be trained by the Council and the training lasted three weeks.

I was apprenticed to a man from Maiden Newton by the name of Bill Clothier, and after he had taught me he offered to take me on for two years. Since then I have never looked back. I was awarded three certificates for thatching and one for teaching, and in my time I have taught about seven others. Most of them didn't keep it up. Jack Osgood was the only one who stuck to it properly. At the age of sixteen he came to me as apprentice from near Salisbury, one of a family of nine, and lived with us until he was married. Since I retired he is the only thatcher in the Piddle Valley and is called on from villages all around, but when I first came there were four other thatchers and we divided the work between us.

When I started house-thatching the cost was 7s. 6d. (37½p) for a ten-foot square of roof. Nowadays the reed alone costs £200 and some odd pounds a time, with spars on top of that. I used to get my spars – spar gads, they are called – off a spar and hurdle-maker called Gale, one of five then in the Valley. They were made of hazel or withy and he used to cut them from hazel coppices on the farms. He kept a lot by him so that there were always some available. They are cut one length, about three feet long, especially for thatching, and when you've got them you split, sharpen and twist them yourself. You use a special hook for this, known as a spar hook and not used for anything else, and make a special twist of your wrist as you split them. Spars have to be cut at the beginning of winter when the sap is going back. For two or three months then you can twist them: if they are cut green they go brittle and aren't suitable for the job. When there is snow or frost you can't thatch, and you spend your time preparing the gads.

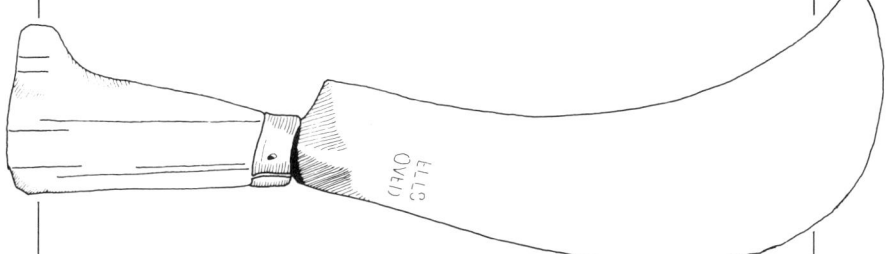

Reeds or wheat-straw are used for thatching, although it is all known as 'reed'. The reeds come from Scotland or Norfolk, and there are some good ones on Radipole Lake, in Weymouth, but I always preferred wheat-straw myself and rarely used anything else. After harvest it is cut on a special machine in just over three-foot lengths. If the reed is too long it wears out quicker, as the ends are more exposed, but even straw that has been through the ordinary threshing machine lasts for about thirty years.

Straw that has pith in it is no good for thatching. After ten years it starts to crack off and you can see every mark of the hook. It also turns black, whereas hollow straw wears better and keeps its colour. I always like to use a variety of wheat called Red Standard but you can't get it now: farmers don't like it because it doesn't give a big enough yield.

You have a special ladder for the job, one that is made inside out. A builder's ladder is straight on the inside and rounded on the outside, but a thatcher's ladder is the opposite way round so that you won't rub your knees while you are working. There is also a hang ladder made with spikes and laid across the thatch up to the ridge. In the old days I had only my push bike, so if a farmer wanted some thatching done I used to get Harry Hawker, the carrier, to take my ladders to Dorchester on top of his van – the 'Flying Bedstead' we called it! – and then the farmer would go to Dorchester to collect them.

If you are thatching a new roof you have to split out a stick, nail it on and then tie the bundles of reeds, known as 'wads', on to the bottom with a length of tarred twine. This keeps the straw ends from falling through. To tie on the twine you use a flat needle about two feet long with a biggish eye. Then you start putting on the thatch. You damp it first, so that it will go together tighter, and start from the bottom, tying it on with the spar gads and tarred twine as you go. You do it right up to the ridge, overlapping each wad by about two-thirds, and moving along from right to left until the whole roof is covered. Each 'coating', as it is called, is nine inches thick, having done the first you do a second, the other way, to make an eighteen-inch thickness. To drive the reeds tightly together you use a 'biddle', a flat bit of wood with ridges on it to clamp against the reed. If you don't 'shut' the reed properly the wet can come in.

When both coatings are on you start at the ridge and come down, trimming off the butts of the reed with a trimming hook. Then you use an eave-hook to cut above the eaves. Some thatchers finish off their work with a design on the ridge, a straw pheasant or such, but I never did. I found that when the rain runs off these fancy bits it makes a gutter all round the roof and spoils the thatch.

Some people like to put wire over the thatch to keep out the birds, but it is expensive. It used to cost 7s. 6d. a roll but now it is between £40 and £50. It certainly helps the thatch to last longer, but if the reed is clean in the first place you don't have much trouble with birds or mice.

Fire is not such a hazard as it used to be. In the old days steam engines were going up and down the Valley and a spark could fly out and set the thatch alight. The old bakehouse in Piddletrenthide was burnt on a bonfire night when a firework landed on the thatch, and only a year ago the Brace of Pheasants in Plush was gutted and the thatch destroyed by fire. The roof has been entirely re-thatched by Jack Osgood and a good job he has made of it. But on the whole the danger of thatch catching fire is not very great.

When I first started work there was a lot of rick thatching to be done. After the harvest, before the corn was threshed, ricks were built with the sheaves of corn and then the thatcher would be called in. Rick thatching was similar to house thatching, although the spars were longer. The corn stayed in the rick to dry for three months and then, when it was ready for threshing, the thatch and spars were taken off to be used on the straw ricks that were built and thatched afterwards.

Nowadays, with the coming of the combine harvester, there are no ricks. Instead, the corn is threshed by the machine and the hay and straw pressed into bales which are tied with baler twine and stacked in barns. During the war house thatching was not allowed, and a chap named Goddard from Cattistock was able to thatch two hundred and odd ricks in one year. The last ricks I thatched were for Mr Paul of Cheselbourne twelve years ago.

I have had very few accidents on the job. Once, thatching a rick at Herrison Hospital, I was going up the ladder with a bundle of reeds over my shoulder when a rung broke and I fell to the ground. I wasn't badly hurt. Another time, working at White's Dairy, Piddlehinton, in the blazing sun I got giddy from the heat and had to come down quick. During the war, rick-thatching at Nether Cerne, I was up on the rick when I saw an aircraft coming straight for me. I could see it was a Messerschmitt. I slid down the rick in double-quick time without bothering about the ladder at all and stayed on the ground until it had gone. Later I heard it had been brought down by one of our fighters not far away.

There have been a lot of changes in the Valley since I came to live here, not all for the better, but thatching itself hasn't changed much, and I suppose it will go on the same as long as there are men to follow the craft. It has been a good life for me, and I reckon I have thatched every thatched house and cottage in the Valley. Lectures and books on thatching are no use: you have to learn by experience. And during my fifty years as a master thatcher I have done just that.

GEORGE HANSFORD

THE MAKING OF A WATTLE HURDLE

Woodmen have been fashioning wattle hurdles from the hazel since the days of the flint axe. But for all its antiquity, hurdle-making lacks the immediate glamour of some rural crafts. The wheelwright's spectacular marriage of ironwork and intricate joinery, ritually consummated in fire, has long fascinated the bystander. His yard, like the forge, was conspicuous in the village. Contrast the hurdle-maker, who must be sought in the loneliness of the woodland which provides his materials. Hurdles, widely used by farmer and gardener alike, are more familiar than the men who make them.

The hurdle-maker is elusive, and his craft might seem unexceptional. The twisting of flexible wooden rods into artefacts is an ancient and primitive technology; weaving hazel into wattle is only a robust form of basketry. No longer used for building in Britain, it has survived in the repetitive craft of hurdle-making. Yet simple technologies are becoming fashionable. A Dorset hurdle-maker uses only a few metal tools, all variants of the billhook. These products of a blacksmith represent his sole essential dependence on any other trade. Raw materials are naturally regenerated, by-products can be adjusted to suit the available markets, and nothing is wasted.

Essential to the craft is the art of splitting each hazel wand down the middle. The available material is thus doubled, and split rods are half the weight of those 'in the round'. They retain adequate strength and, most important of all, can be twisted without breaking to double back on themselves. The splitting process is far from easy and requires long practice: some forgotten genius must have devised it. Experiments have shown that the iron age 'sickle' of archaeology, so ineffectual an implement for reaping corn, is ideal for splitting hazel, so the hurdle-maker's spar hook has a long lineage.

The rod is held in the left hand and the sharp steel snicked into a fork at the slender end to start the cleft. If no such fork exists, long practice guides the blade into the side of the wand to sink only halfway through it. The rod is fed steadily into the keen edge, which slides through the creaking fibres as the haft is twisted to force the clean white wood apart. Pressure is applied to the left or right, as required, to steady the blade's central course despite the irregularities in the timber conspiring to divert it.

Like all crafts, hurdle-making has plenty of technical terms. Local dialects, the isolated nature of the work, and its extreme antiquity, have conspired to proliferate them. In Dorset the hurdle is made by weaving the 'split rods' in and out of the vertical stakes known as 'sails'. The sails – ten for a standard sheep hurdle – are held in position during construction by a stout piece of timber called a 'flake'. This is pegged to the ground and bored with holes to accommodate them.

As the hurdle-maker fells a stool, using a different bill-hook from his sparhook, he segregates the miscellany of material to meet his future needs. The two outer sails are always round stakes; the rest may be whole or cleft according to personal style or the availability of suitable timber. The feathery tips of the hazel wands, formerly bound as faggots for the bread ovens, can now be sold as peasticks. A straight stem of suitable diameter may yield a two foot six 'gad' at the butt, to be cleft in half and half again to give four thatching spars, the remainder making two split rods. Stouter stems, unsuitable for splitting, may be sold as beanpoles, neatly tied into bundles with a strand of hazel. Even the dead wood provides fuel; and in bitter weather a fire can thaw the frozen hazel to make it pliant.

As he gathers his harvest, the woodman is maintaining the coppice, that it may yield him quality material at the next rotation. Properly cut stools will last for generations; if one should finally rot a naturally planted seedling may replace it. Failing that, the hurdle-maker will bend down a stem from a neighbouring stool and bury the tip, which will take root and fill the gap.

It is surprising how much material a single stool provides, and a man may work conveniently from one place for many days as he clears the area around him. The outdoor workshop is simple but efficient. Next to the flake, a short, stout post is driven into the ground, for severing gads and sharpening the sails, using yet another billhook. Rods to be split are neatly stacked to hand with their butts resting on a horizontal pole or 'gallows', supported on two neighbouring stools. With ten sails driven into the flake with a billet of timber, construction can begin. The bottom few inches of the hurdle are woven from round hazel, of smaller diameter, which is easier to intertwine than split material. Several rods are started between the inner sails, woven in and out to the extremities, and doubled back to continue the weave. The wattle is so contrived that, as in a basket, all the ends of the rods are safely tucked in away from the bottom edge of the hurdle, and so woven into their successors that they cannot slip downwards off the sails. The pattern is intricate and twisting the rods round the outermost sails is a real art, requiring both skill and strength in the wrist. The wooden fibres are separated like the strands of a rope, which can each bend round the sail without breaking.

Once started the work proceeds rapidly, rods being taken from the gallows and split as required. The weave is compacted periodically with a leather-padded knee or hand. It looks easy, but there is much skill in keeping the sails straight to avoid warp in the finished product. The holes in a flake in fact lie on a gentle curve, helping to stabilize the half-built hurdle. The split rods will bend a little as they dry out, tightening the wattle and compensating for the original bias.

True sheep hurdles have a lens-shaped gap, divided by the exposed sails, woven into their middles. Several can be threaded on to a stout pole and carried on the shepherd's shoulder. But the bulk of production today is destined for suburban gardens, and the weave continues uniformly to the top. Here again, an ingenious intertwining of the last few rods binds each into the body of the hurdle and secures the ends.

The weaving is complete and a hurdle hook is used to trim back the protruding butts. Neatly shorn, the finished hurdle is lifted from the flake and laid to dry atop its predecessors. Each is virtually identical, and the resulting stack has a regularity and symmetry of form to delight the eye.

GEORGE DARWALL

COPPICING AND HURDLE-MAKING *

The ride shone pink with gossamer in the early summer sun
and my feet were drenched with dew. A rustle from the
brambles stayed my soft progress through the Dorset
wood. I froze as the briar was tugged by an unseen creature,
less than three yards from me. Long seconds later a roebuck
stepped into view, fox-russet in the dawn, wet black nose
tasting the air and burnished antlers proudly erect. He
paused a moment on the track, culled another succulent
shoot and vanished as mysteriously as he had come.

I have seldom been closer to a wild deer, but my triumph
was tinged with sadness. The buck embodied life and vita-
lity, but the wood itself was dying. Like a decaying farm
wagon it was obsolete, a relic of a former system, no longer
functional but nevertheless demanding respect for the
craftsmen who fashioned it.

Hazel woods were planted for sheep, not deer. The flocks
which buttressed the wealth of Wessex were folded on the
downs with hurdles: cleft ash in the north and woven hazel
in the south. Acres of woodland were cut in rotation every
seven years or so, and the natural capacity of hazel to regenerate from a 'stool' ensured a continuous crop. This
process of 'coppicing' provided the straight stems cun-
ningly split and entwined by the hurdlemaker in the woods.

His art is best appreciated through personal experiment.
Borrow his keen billhook and try splitting a hazel wand
from end to end yourself. If this defeats you, respect a man
who can feel the blade down the stem without watching his
hands. Marvel at his speed and dexterity when cleaving
shorter lengths into quadrants, to form the pointed sticks
known as 'spars'. These will be twisted in the iron grip of
the thatcher and thrust deep into a roof to pin down the
straw. Remember the villages of the Piddle Valley which
are thus dependent on hazel.

A few hurdlers still make a living from garden screens for
suburbia, but sheep farming has changed. Hurdles are as
outmoded as thatched roofs, and many of the hazel woods

* Taken from the prize-winning entry for the 1977 Kenneth Allsop
Memorial Essay Competition by kind permission of the *Sunday Times*.

stand neglected and overgrown. My morning walk led me through stools cut for the last time and poisoned, dispossessed by the ranks of usurping conifers.

Don't blame the landowner for changes forced by hard commercial fact. There is little demand for hazel as a crop and it is left uncut. Some is temporarily reprieved by the pheasant; the rest is inevitably replaced by more profitable timber.

Why mourn the coppice anyway? Is it merely sentiment at the passing of an ancient craft and a form of land use no longer economic? Alas, it is the loss not only of the beautiful woodlands themselves but of the plants and animals which inhabit them. Deer will survive at least the early stages of replanting with conifers; many creatures will not. Coppices are an immensely rich and varied habitat, far more beneficial to wildlife than modern forestry plantations. On the open areas, cleared by the woodman this winter, may be found spectacular displays of bluebells and violets next spring. But the prime feature of coppice is its stability. Next year, after the hurdler's billhook has taken its crop, nothing will have changed. A graduation from open space to closed canopy will remain, giving variation in perpetuity.

It is the diversity of hazel woods as a habitat, and the fact of their rapid disappearance, which has moved conservation bodies to maintain some coppices as nature reserves, retaining the traditional pattern of rotational cropping. This requires labour, and there is little money to pay for it. Consequently many areas of woodland are now being coppiced by volunteers. Such workers have neither the time nor the expertise to make hurdles, but even cutting the poles demands skill; the stems should be cleanly severed at an angle so that the rain will run off and the stump can regenerate without rotting. The art comes only with practice.

The very nature of such work, at first sight apparently destructive, is a revelation to the more narrow-minded 'nature lover'. Hazel woods are best maintained by periodically cutting them down. But are volunteers in coppices killing off the professional hurdle-maker altogether? Far from it. There is, paradoxically, too much hazel at present, and many woodlands are overgrown and not attractive to the few remaining craftsmen. Alternative coppices, like the territory of my roebuck, are being cropped for the last time and will not be allowed to regenerate. Nature reserves, properly managed, could provide the material for a few hurdlers and thatchers indefinitely.

A gang of volunteers can descend on a wood and cut a great deal of hazel in a weekend. The same area would occupy a hurdler for months. He would be obtaining raw material, maintaining the woodland through enlightened self-interest, and incidentally preserving the flora and fauna. Conservation workers may cover their costs by selling bean-poles; they will never achieve the economic production of professionals. As the acreage of coppice dwindles the demand for what is left should rise, provided there is still room in a modern society for garden screens and thatched roofs. The amateurs who have bridged the gap and looked after the woods in the meantime can stand aside. The overgrown stools they are cutting now will be yielding quality poles in seven years' time.

So let us hope that a few hurdle-makers will continue to follow their ancient craft and make a living from hazelwoods. Your garden fence could subsidize a beautiful natural world and ensure that the next generation may watch the deer among the bluebells.

GEORGE DARWALL

COTTAGE INDUSTRY

Not many people, even those living in the Valley, know that an unusual and fascinating cottage industry is carried on in Piddletrenthide. It started about eight years ago when my brother-in-law, the owner of a sports business in Australia, came over to England to buy nets, or pockets, for his billiard tables. The firm that had supplied him in the past were three years behind with their deliveries and he was urgently trying to find another source of supply.

I happened to mention the position to Betty Hunt, whose mother-in-law had made camouflage netting during the war.

'I can't make the pockets myself,' said Mrs Hunt, 'but my

sister in Beaminster can. If you would like me to teach you the braiding I'll get her to tell you how to make the actual nets.'

From this almost casual beginning the industry started.

The nets are made with a piece of wood, a needle and some cotton twine. You tie a length of the twine round a table leg or on a hook, cast on and make a row of large knots over the wood to form the tassel at the bottom. You braid on from there and join it up. Although it sounds reasonably simple, the actual braiding stitch is very difficult to learn if you have never done it before. For ring or rail pockets for snooker tables you work in the same way but cast the twine on to a brass ring.

The pockets are made in sets of six and vary in size according to the size of the billiard table. The string comes from a Bridport net manufacturer. At one time it was difficult to get the proper cotton twine and the company supplied us with nylon instead, but it was not so satisfactory and now we are back to cotton twine again.

From the first, orders from Australia flooded in. At one time we had as many as 45 ladies making the nets and altogether I taught 120 people to do the work. When production was at its height we supplied 150 sets a month. Of course the demand fluctuated. Christmas was the busiest time and to supply that demand we had to send the sets off in August, for the journey by sea might take anything from two to four months, although at the beginning we had to air freight them as my brother-in-law was desperate for them. Altogether, we must have sent hundreds and hundreds, pretty well all of them from Piddletrenthide Post Office. Today, with less demand, we send one parcel a month. Sadly Taiwan has taken over most of the trade, although my brother-in-law still prefers our nets because he says the bottoms don't fall out of them!

Although the work is not well paid, it is a useful addition to the income of those ladies who are not able to go out to work. Nine or ten of them still do it. It takes them about three-quarters of an hour to make one pocket, but at least they can watch television while they are braiding!

HELEN COOPER

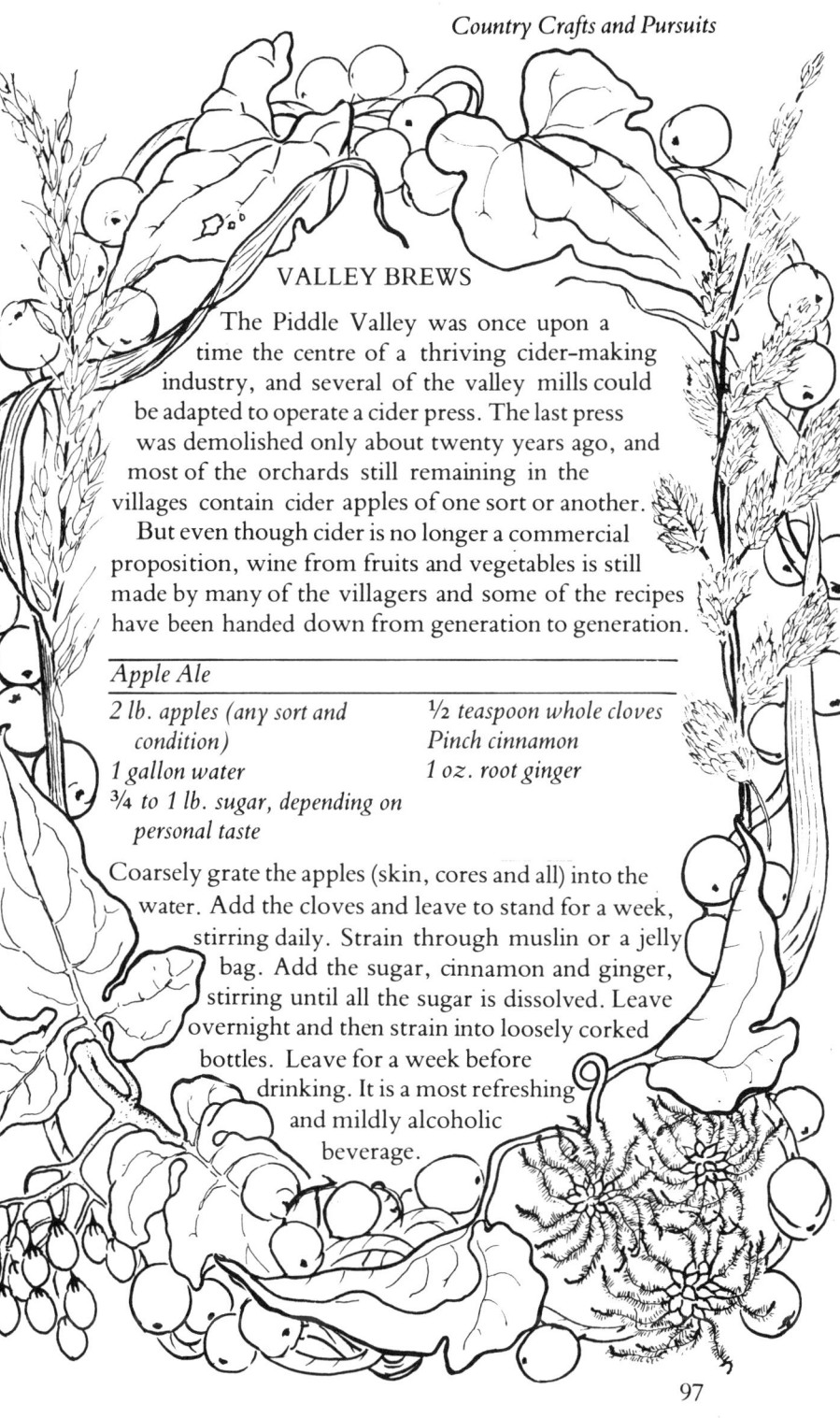

VALLEY BREWS

The Piddle Valley was once upon a time the centre of a thriving cider-making industry, and several of the valley mills could be adapted to operate a cider press. The last press was demolished only about twenty years ago, and most of the orchards still remaining in the villages contain cider apples of one sort or another. But even though cider is no longer a commercial proposition, wine from fruits and vegetables is still made by many of the villagers and some of the recipes have been handed down from generation to generation.

Apple Ale

2 lb. apples (any sort and condition)
1 gallon water
¾ to 1 lb. sugar, depending on personal taste

½ teaspoon whole cloves
Pinch cinnamon
1 oz. root ginger

Coarsely grate the apples (skin, cores and all) into the water. Add the cloves and leave to stand for a week, stirring daily. Strain through muslin or a jelly bag. Add the sugar, cinnamon and ginger, stirring until all the sugar is dissolved. Leave overnight and then strain into loosely corked bottles. Leave for a week before drinking. It is a most refreshing and mildly alcoholic beverage.

Sloe Gin

Fill a wine bottle or large jar three-quarters full of ripe sloes which have been pricked all over to let the juice run out. Purists say you should use a silver needle, but a darning needle or even a pair of scissors is just as effective and far less fiddly. Add 4 to 6 ounces of granulated sugar, depending on how sweet you like your liqueur, and then fill the whole bottle with gin. Shake it every day for a fortnight until the sugar is quite dissolved. Try to leave it for at least six months before drinking.

Pea Pod Wine

4 lb. pea pods	*1 gallon water*
3½ lb. sugar	*¾ oz. baker's yeast*
1 lemon	

Boil the pea pods with the thinly pared rind of the lemon until tender. Strain on to the sugar and stir well. When lukewarm, add the yeast mixed with a small quantity of the warm liquid and also add the juice of the lemon. Stir and leave in a warm place for 24 hours. Make sure it is well covered. Strain into a clean fermenting jar and insert the air lock. Leave to ferment to a finish in a warm place. Allow to clear and then bottle. The longer it is kept the better it tastes.

Elderflower Champagne

1½ lb. sugar	*10 large heads of elderflowers*
2 tablespoons white wine	*1 gallon cold water*
vinegar	*2 lemons*

Put the sugar and vinegar into a very large bowl. To this add the elderflower heads and the cold water. Squeeze and quarter the lemons and add them with their juice to the mixture. Let it stand for 24 hours, stirring occasionally. Strain before bottling into screwtop bottles. It is ready to drink after a few days.

Elderberry Wine

4 lb. elderberries	*juice of a lemon*
½ lb. chopped sultanas	*3 lb. sugar*
4 oz. chopped raisins	*¾ oz. yeast*

Crush the elderberries, and put them with chopped sultanas and raisins into a bucket. Add the lemon juice and 2 pints of boiled, cooled water. Soak 4 to 6 hours. Dissolve 2 lb. sugar in 2 pints water over a gentle heat and then bring to the boil. Boil for 2 minutes. Add this syrup with ¾ oz. yeast to the bucket and leave covered for 3 days only. Strain into a clean bucket and leave covered for 5 more days. Dissolve 1 lb. sugar in 2 pints water over a gentle heat, boil and cool. Add this to the must in the bucket together with some yeast nutrient, bought from the chemist. Pour into a demijohn (if necessary fill to the top with cool boiled water) and fix the lock. Leave in a warm place to ferment. Rack as required and bottle when clear.

Blackberry Wine

3 lb. blackberries	*1 level teaspoon pectinaze*
12 oz. chopped sultanas	*1 level teaspoon yeast nutrient*
3 lb. sugar	*¾ oz. yeast*

Put blackberries, sultanas and 2 lb. sugar into a bucket. Boil 7 pints of water and pour over. Cover and leave for 3 days. Add pectinaze, yeast nutrient and yeast (all bought from the chemist). Stir. Leave for 4 days. Stir in 1 lb. sugar. Leave for 7 days. Sieve, pour into a demi–john and fit the lock. Leave in a warm place to ferment. Rack as required and bottle when clear.

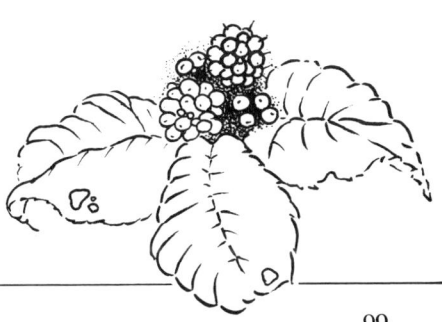

Church Customs *

THE DUTIES OF CHURCHWARDENS

Soon after Christmas the clergy start thinking about Annual Meetings. Before I came to the Piddle Valley I had had to deal with only one Annual Meeting a year and even this I always found something of a strain. But now that I have four to contend with, as do most country clergy these days, the yearly chore moves from the near impossible to the ridiculous. Parishioners do not always appreciate the fact that the Annual Meeting in fact consists of two clearly defined meetings. The first is to elect the churchwardens for the ensuing twelve months. This meeting may be attended by those on the Church Electoral Roll and also by any resident who is on the Register of Local Government Electors. The appointment of the churchwardens, certainly of one of them, may thus be influenced by people who have no religious beliefs at all or who may even be Moslems or Hindus or anything else you care to mention.

To deal with such a situation there is a built-in safeguard dating from 1604 to the effect that, if the incumbent disapproves of a candidate, he can make his own appointment; in other words a reversion to the old system of People's Warden and Vicar's Warden. Fortunately the safeguard is rarely used. The reason for this somewhat anomalous state of affairs can be traced back into the past, when churchwardens held enormous power, and so it seemed right that

---

* From a sermon preached by the Rev. Derek Parry, Vicar of the Piddle Valley.

the community as a whole should have a say in the choice of candidate.

In medieval times, of course, the Parish Church held a central position in the life of the community. The church building was used as a parish hall. Ale was brewed on the premises and sold for church funds, and often drunk during dances and fairs held in the churchyard. And so, because the church was the centre of communal life, the churchwardens were extremely busy men. They had to keep accounts of everything connected with the finances of the church, and this included the distribution of relief to the needy. They also had to collect the rents from land and other property left to the church. As recently as 1974 my predecessor had to collect rents as part of his stipend, but fortunately this practice was discontinued when he left. The churchwardens had to care for the church cattle. They had to sell wool and cheese and gifts in kind made to the church. They had to organize church 'ales', rural festivals so called because the chief diversion was the consumption of ale. It was also their duty to prosecute such offenders against ecclesiastical law as adulterers and sabbath breakers. And, as if that was not enough to keep them out of mischief, they were expected to act as bankers and pawn-brokers and were liable for the safe custody of the maypole and of the bells and coats used by the Morris dancers.

After the Reformation they had yet more civil duties to perform: the provision of arms for the militia; the relief of married soldiers; and the provision of pounds for stray cattle and stocks and pillories for the punishment of wrong-doers. To fill up any spare moments they were also responsible for the destruction of vermin.

A few extracts from the Piddlehinton Churchwardens' Accounts recorded at the end of the seventeenth century and the beginning of the eighteenth show just what busy men they were and what a variety of duties fell to their lot. The entries sound even more remote and unusual because of the spelling which in those far-off days was a matter of personal choice rather than of accepted standard:

1686
Pd to one of the King's souldiers who was wounded
and disbanded   6d.
Given to a woman & three children who were undon
by fire in the West India licensed to ask relief   1s. 0d.

1687
Given to a woman and her children lisensed who
came out of Ireland undon by fire   7d.
July 16 Paid Joan Skinner for cutting the nettles in
the churchyard   4d.
Nov 15 John Runnier for 1 dozen of sparros heads   1d.
Nov 17 Paid John Day for a pollcats head   4d
Paid David Day for a stoats head   2d.

1688
Given to the Ringers at the Princes birth day   2d.
Given to a man & his wife & five small children
undon by an earthquake   1d.
Given to 3 men that came out of Ireland their ship
cast away   10d.
Given to a man that came out of Turky that had but
one hand   6d.

1689
For washing ye surplice twice   2s. 0d.
To a parcel of seamen licensed to travel   2s. 0d.

1694
paid A man which ye French boorned [burned]   1s. 0d.

1695
Gave a seaman wife towards ye rejoining of her
husban out of Turky   6d.
Paid 4 seamen taken by ye French & exchanged   1s. 6d.
Paid for bread and wine Against Chrismas   5s. 2d.
Gave 11 wounded seamen   2s. 0d.
Gave a man, 3 women, 2 children taken by ye
French   1s. 0d.

1698
Given a lame man that his leg did rot   3d.
Given to a sea man who had lost his ship   3d.
Given to John Day for hedghogg heads   1d.

1745
8 December Gave a poore woman and three children
  who came throe this parrish late and was not able
  able to go no further   7d.

1749
4 September for keping 6 children 1 wick   8s. 0d.

1752
18 September Paid William Cevet for a polcat   4d.
3 October paid William Soams for a stoat head   2d.
paid clerk salary for washing ye lining [linen]   5s. 4d.
Paid him for atending ye clock and oyl   5s. 4d.

1763
Paid at the Archduckns visatshon [Archdeacon's
  Visitation]   3s. 6d.

1764
Paid for a Toon and half of tiles for ye porch   16s. 6d.
Going to by ye Tiles   11s. 0d.

1762
Paid for a prayer Boock and the Kings prockle-
  matshon   1s. 10d.

1766
Paid for 14 doz sparos   1s. 2d.
4 stots   8d.
10 doz sparos   4d.
bread and wine   3s. 5d.

Although these are random extracts from the churchwardens' earliest account book, they show that a great
many of the disbursements were paid to destitute men and
women arriving in the parish. They also show that in a
number of cases the recipients are described as 'licensed'.
Under an Elizabethan law, itinerant folk travelling through
the countryside in search of work, or perhaps making their
way home after a spell at sea or in the army, were issued
with a licence or pass enabling them to obtain relief from the
parishes through which they made their way. It is not
difficult to visualize them: destitute and perhaps deserted
women dragging themselves around the country with their
children; sick men; wounded soldiers; shipwrecked sailors –
all asking for alms and receiving the few pence which today

seem trivial but 400 years ago meant the difference between life and death.

With regard to vermin, it is interesting to note that the polecat, which features frequently in the list of payments, is now virtually extinct throughout the British Isles except for central Wales and a few corners of Devon. Sparrows, whose heads were brought in by the hundred, must have done great harm to corn and thatch, and so there was a price, albeit a small one, for each bundle of them brought to the churchwardens. Hedgehogs and stoats, now known to be entirely harmless to man, were also considered worthy of a capitation (or decapitation!) grant.

Needless to say, the churchwardens of today are not called upon to discharge many of the tasks mentioned above, but their duties are still very important. They have legal status for a start. They are the officers of the Bishop, and this is why they escort him, with their wands of office, when he visits the church. Churchwardens' wands are often tipped with a mitre for the Vicar's Warden and a crown for the People's Warden, thus emphasizing their specific loyalties. They must keep order in the church and churchyard, and they have the right to arrest any person who behaves in a riotous manner and bring him before the magistrates. By various acts of Parliament they must provide registers and service books and ensure the safety of the communion plate. Indeed, the churchwardens are the legal owners of the goods and ornaments of the church. If there is an interregnum or the Vicar is ill or is sent to gaol, it is the duty of the wardens to take over most of his responsibilities.

So the first of the two Annual Meetings is to appoint the churchwardens. The second is the Annual Parochial Church Meeting at which reports are given and the new Parochial Church Council is elected. As this is a purely church affair, those present who are not on the church electoral roll can be asked to leave. The PCC is a comparatively new invention (it was given legal status in 1921), and it took over many of the duties and responsibilities hitherto held by the churchwardens. It also provided the laity with an element of democracy and a share in parochial administration. Its primary duty is 'to co-operate with the incumbent in promoting in the parish the whole mission of the church, pastoral, evangelistic, social and ecumenical.' It further has the legal right to impose a rate on all church members in order to meet church expenses, although this rate is voluntary and seldom levied.

'BURIED IN WOOL'

The burial entries in the Piddletrenthide Church Register between the years 1679 and 1704 contain what might seem at first glance peculiar and even irrelevant information. For instance:

Anno Dom. 1679
Samuel ye Son of Samuel Strickland was buried in woolen ye 4th of April – certificate on file numb. 1.
Jane ye daughter of James Bollen buried in woollen ye 10 of September – certificate on file numb. 4.
John Shepherd ye elder was buried in woollen ye 18 September – certificate on file numb. 5.
Anne the wife of James Bollen was buryed in wollin November 6th – 8

The existence of these entries – and each of the hundreds of them is similar apart from the spelling of the word 'woollen', variously and delightfully rendered as 'woolen', 'wollen', 'wollin', 'wolland', 'wooling' and 'woll' – reflects the story of England's rise to greatness as a wool-producing power and also her gradual decline; it vividly demonstrates how the country's history can be traced in some measure through the church registers of a small Dorset village.

The English way of life, it has been said, was carried into the world on the back of a sheep, and certainly the foundation and backbone of Britain's commerce was the wool trade. It was the excellence of that wool – perhaps a result of climatic conditions – which gave the country a premier place in the markets of Europe, and for centuries the great flocks of sheep that roamed the fields and hillsides were the most important part of Britain's economy.

Sheep were grazed before the coming of the Romans, and their skins and wool almost certainly used for clothing and shelter, although they were a somewhat different breed from those familiar to us today. The Romans in their turn established a wool factory at Winchester in the year AD 80 to provide warm clothing for the occupying troops more used to the sunshine of Italy than the cold, damp climate of Britain. It was in the Middle Ages, however, that the wool trade reached its peak. Wool had been exported to the Continent for some time and there woven into cloth by the skilful weavers of Flanders, but in 1100 a party of Flemings, driven out of Flanders by floods, obtained permission to settle in England and carry on their trade. Now the cloth-makers themselves were on English soil. 'All the nations of the world,' wrote Matthew of Westminster, pseudonym of the unknown author of *Flores Historiarum*, 'were kept warm by the wool of England made into cloth by the men of Flanders.'

In due course the weaving industry became one of the most important in the country, and the famous 'wool churches' of East Anglia and elsewhere are a testimony to the wealth and prosperity brought by wool. From time to time, embargoes were placed on its export in order to safeguard the home trade. These were always rescinded later, but in the middle of the seventeenth century a law was passed entirely forbidding the export of wool. This Act remained on the Statute Book, in fact if not in actual practice, for over 100 years.

Contrary to hopes and expectations, the new law was disastrous for the wool trade: the price of raw wool fell; smuggling between England and the Continent became an organized traffic; the whole industry deteriorated, and sheep farmers and weavers found themselves out of work and poverty-stricken.

Bizarre acts were passed in order to stimulate demand and provide work for the weavers again. In 1678 the Burial in Woollens Act was put on the Statute Book, and it is this Act which was responsible for the strange entries in the Piddle-trenthide Church Register.

The Act laid down that everyone, rich and poor alike, was to be buried in a woollen shroud; in order to make sure that the law was obeyed a certificate had to be issued to that effect. Failure to comply with the law incurred a £5 fine – a considerable sum in those days. Informers were persuaded to denounce any defaulters by being awarded half the fine. The parson also received a portion of it and the residue went to the Government.

The parishioners of Piddletrenthide seem to have been a conformist body, for there is no mention in the register of the payment of any fine. Every one of the hundreds of corpses was buried in wool. By 1690, the original deposition of a 'certificate' had been changed to an 'affidavit'. After the year 1704 no actual mention of wool occurs, although the word 'affidavit' is still written in:

Anno Domini 1683
Sarah ye wife of Richard Dumberfield was buried in wollin Oct 12 – Cert. since ye Visitacon of ye Bp.
Mary ye wife of Dan Dumberfield was buried in Wollen Aug 4 – Certif.
Rich. Dumberfield the Elder was buryed in wollen March 24 – cert.

1691
Mary Squibb was buryed in wollen – affid Apr 1 after the Chancelors visitaon

1693
Daniel Dumberfield was buryed in wollen – affidavit dated the 12th day of February

1704
William and Mary ye children of William Bollen was boureyed Aprill ye 22 day in woollen – afit datted Aprill ye 24th.

One cannot help wondering if the Bishop and Chancellor made their 'visitacon' in order to make sure that the Burial in Woollens Act was being observed to the letter. No doubt some influential people managed to wriggle out of it. High-born and wealthy men and women would not have relished the thought of being wrapped in such a menial shroud. Alexander Pope, in his poem 'The Rape of the Lock', can have the last word:

> 'Odious! in woollens! 'twould a saint provoke!'
> Were the last words that poor Narcissa spoke.
> 'No: let a charming chintz and Brussels lace
> Wrap my cold limbs and shade my lifeless face.'

SHROVE-TIDE

On Shrove Tuesday in the old days bands of children would call at the houses and cottages in the Valley begging for titbits and singing their 'Shroving Song':

> Here we come a-shroving
> For a piece of pancake
> And a little truckle cheese
> Of your own making.
> Hot pot the pan's hot,
> The butter door is open,
> Pray missus, good missus,
> If your heart be open
> Here we come without our bag
> Afraid we shan't get nothing.

A truckle cheese was a small round cheese made of sour milk and weighing about a pound, so called because it could be rolled or truckled along the ground.

The children would be given an egg, an apple, a piece of cheese or a pancake, but sometimes the bigger boys would arm themselves with potsherds, old pans and broken china which they would throw at the door if they were turned away without a gift.

It has been suggested that 'Lent-crocking' – pelting the doors of ungenerous villagers with broken crockery – was symbolic in ancient times of the approach of Ash Wednesday and the Lenten fast. For forty days meat would not be eaten, and so the unwanted pots and pans must be thrown away. Other sources suggest that getting rid of the broken china signified the discarding of sin and the beginning of a new and more wholesome life.

The custom of 'shriving' was revived in Piddlehinton some years ago by the wife of the then rector, Archdeacon Chute, with the help of the Mothers' Union. On Shrove Tuesday they went to church to confess their sins and then gathered in the kitchen of the Rectory – now Glebe House – to hold a pancake party and dance round the table before Ash Wednesday and the season of Lent.

ROGATION SUNDAY

On this Sunday, the fifth before Easter, the ancient custom of walking round the perimeter of the parish and blessing the crops – sometimes called 'beating the bounds' – is still carried on in the village of Plush. The vicar, churchwardens and parishioners make their way, nowadays by car although formerly they used to walk, to the outlying farms in order to ask for God's blessing on the crops and also to preserve the rights and properties of the parish. They sing hymns to the music of a recorder, say prayers and then return to the little church for a final blessing.

The milkwort (*Polygala vulgaris*) with its blue, white or pink petals is the Rogation flower and was once made into garlands and carried in the Rogation procession. If it blooms abundantly farmers say there will be a good harvest.

PALM SUNDAY

On Palm Sunday, the next before Easter, which celebrates the triumphant entry of Christ into Jerusalem, palms in the shape of crosses are distributed to the church congregations of the Valley in memory of the palm branches which were strewed before His path.

VERSES FROM THE VICARAGE

Taxing The Vicar

> To the Tax Man he never has lied
> So he wondered just what was implied
> When this year the request
> For his tax was addressed
> To The Vicarage, Fiddletrenthide.

Rustic Reward

> 'I've brought a little gift for you,'
> A small boy said to me.
> 'A sort of "thank you" present
> As I often come to tea.
>
> 'I only found it yesterday.'
> Whatever could it be?
> 'I do hope you will like it –
> It's a baby toad,' said he.

Piddletrenthide Church Fete

> Crowds were coming in faster and thicker.
> As I stood watching sales getting quicker
> A small boy at my side
> When asked: 'Who's she?' replied,
> 'That's the lady who lives with the Vicar.'

HEATHER PARRY

Witchcraft, Ghosts, Legends and Superstitions

THE WITCH OF PIDDLEHINTON

Many years ago, some of the old inhabitants of Piddle-hinton used to tell me stories, passed down by their fore-fathers, about witches who once lived in the Piddle Valley.

One such story concerns an old lady who lived in Piddle-hinton and whom the locals regarded as a witch. She lived in a thatched cottage which had very dark passages and was dimly lit. Whenever anyone knocked on her door she refused to answer it, and so any visitors had to fumble their way up the eerie passages into her living-room. There she would be curled up in a big arm chair with her toes sticking out of the tops of her black boots and a black cat sitting on her lap. She roamed the village at all hours of the night and was very rarely seen during the day time. Whether it was night or day, the old folks used to tell me, you could hear her coming from quite a distance because the bottom of her long black skirt would whistle and brush itself against the ground. She had wizened and pointed features, with long, gnarled fingers and hands. It is said that people were so frightened of her that they would sooner 'run a mile and jump a stile' than pass her in the street. It was also said that at the swish of her besom stick she could turn herself into a hare or other small animal. A hare would often be seen haunting the downs and hills of the village, and the locals were in no doubt that it was in fact the old witch. The hare was so canny that it was impossible to shoot it. Local tradition said that a 'witch hare' could only be effectively disposed of if it were shot at dead of night and this was, of course, an almost hopeless task.

On one moonlit night as the local squire was riding at a gallop through the village, his horse accidentally kicked a hare. The squire jumped off his horse in an attempt to catch the animal, but he was not quick enough and it limped away into the night. A few days later the witch woman could be seen hobbling about the village, while the hare was also observed limping across the downs and hills. Both witch and hare remained thus crippled for the rest of their lives.

GEOFFREY LORD

To Avoid the Evil Eye

Ralph Wightman recorded this charm to avoid being 'over-looked' by a witch: tie a knot of mountain ash [rowan] into a cross and thread it through the hairs of a cow's tail. This will ward off the evil eye.

To Cure an Animal Bewitched

Take a bullock's heart, stick the thorns of gorse or hawthorn into it and set it before the fire. As it begins to scorch, the power of the witch starts to diminish. When it finally bursts with the heat, the spell is broken.

A broom placed across the door will keep witches out.

But to bring certain plants into the house is courting disaster. Blackthorn, 'leyloc' (Dorset for white lilac) and 'fuz' (Dorset for gorse or furze) should never cross the threshold, or ill luck will surely follow.

THE VICARAGE GHOSTS

The building which seems to harbour more ghosts than any other in the Valley is the vicarage at Piddletrenthide. Both Derek and Heather Parry, the Vicar and his wife, and their sons Marcus and Nicholas, take the existence of these phenomena for granted: inexplicable noises; lights that turn off without the help of a human hand; footsteps that are not made by a human foot. Sometimes the ghosts are mischievous and irritating. Heather Parry is often working in the kitchen when she glimpses through the hatch a flickering, shadowy something which is so distracting that she has been known to say crossly: 'Oh, do go *away!*'

The rest of the family agrees that 'something lives in the dining-room.' Marcus describes it as 'a black blob'. Heather has often felt it in front of the hearth. A young guest, going up to the fireplace, said: 'I don't much like it here,' and would only be pacified when his hostess went to stand beside him. As soon as she moved away he hurriedly moved away, too.

'My theory,' says Heather, 'is that it is the ghost of a rather austere clergyman who intimidates small children. And can't you just see him, warming his back in front of the fire as so many men do!'

There has recently been considerable demolition work carried out in the vicarage and the family believes that the ghosts have been disturbed by it. It is then that people in the house experience the noises, the footsteps and the strange sensation of a presence close by. As soon as the work comes to an end or rebuilding takes the place of demolition, the ghosts retire.

One evening Marcus and Nicholas went to see how the work was progressing. Coming back along an upstairs corridor they forgot to turn off the lights. Their mother came up the stairs as they appeared, and to her stupefaction the lights were suddenly turned off behind them. Had a fuse gone? They went to inspect, but the switch was in perfect order.

On another occasion the family had cause to be sincerely grateful to one of the ghosts. They smelled burning in the drawing-room, rushed in and found a large patch of carpet in front of the fire smouldering. But the coal, still red-hot, that had caused the burn had been carefully put back in the hearth where it could do no more damage. 'There is no way,' says the Vicar, 'in which it could have jumped back in the fireplace of its own accord.'

It is not only the Parry family who are conscious of the presence of unseen beings in the vicarage. The builders have also encountered them. One of them, drinking tea in the kitchen beside the cooker, suddenly 'jumped two feet in the air'. 'There was something standing there,' he told Mrs Parry, 'and I felt cold up to my knees.'

Many years before these events took place, two other workmen also experienced something they could not explain. Bill Hunt and Charles Harvey were doing a job for Bill Park: it was demolition again, for they were dismantling a wall in one of the downstairs rooms. Bill Hunt heard Mr Park walking down the passage outside.

'Is Bill coming, then?' he asked.

No one appeared and so he opened the door and peered out, but there was no one there.

'We looked at one another,' says Mr Hunt. "There was a ghost gone by," I said to Charlie, and I was never comfortable working there afterwards.'

Half a century later, Mr Hunt still insists: 'I heard the footsteps plain as plain, but Bill Park hadn't been near the vicarage all day.'

Lights and footsteps, noises and strange sensations, these are the different phenomena described as 'supernatural'. But the apparition seen by the Vicar himself is something else altogether. In Derek Parry's own words:

'The time of the year was mid-August and I was alone in bed, the rest of the family having gone on holiday. It was getting light, around five o'clock in the morning. I am one of those people who wake up quickly; I don't take a long time to do it; I am either asleep or very wide awake. Suddenly I woke up and there at the bottom of the bed was this clergyman. I saw him quite clearly. It was not a vague thing that might have been a wardrobe or something like that glimpsed in the half light. My immediate reaction was: it's a ghost. My second reaction, coming very quickly after the first, was: how surprising that I'm not afraid. Somehow I thought that I ought to be. He stood at the foot of the bed, looking slightly to his left and not at me, with a rather melancholy expression on his face. He was bareheaded, wearing rather old-fashioned clothes – a conventional suit but with somewhat sloping shoulders and a deep "dog collar" – the whole impression being of someone after the turn of the century, between 1900 and the 1920s. He stood there and I stared and stared, continuing to think what an absolutely staggering thing it was and also how amazing that I was not afraid. There was no feeling of cold, no unpleasant smell, no cause for fear. Perhaps if it had been the ghost of a bishop I might have felt differently! For at least ten seconds I stared, perhaps longer. I remember thinking to myself: "How should I deal with this?" In the end, I switched on the bedside light and immediately it disappeared. I have never seen it since.'

It is, of course, not easy to decide if it was, in fact, the ghost of a past vicar of Piddletrenthide that Derek Parry encountered or, if so, which vicar it could have been. The Rev. C.W. H.Dicker (1905–13) is the most obvious contender. He was an interesting and talented man, and his tragic death (he was run over and killed by a steam lorry) might in some way have caused his ghost to walk. The dates are right, but in photographs Mr Dicker is always seen wearing a beard, whereas Mr Parry's visitor was clean shaven.

The matter remains, as they say in the Scottish courts, unproven. But that there are presences which haunt the vicarage and can be seen and heard and felt there can be little, if any, doubt.

THE MANOR HOUSE GHOST

Mr Bill Hunt's aunt used to work in the Manor House at Piddletrenthide, and on more than one occasion she heard the rustle of skirts behind her. Turning round, she would catch a glimpse of a lady in a long silk dress who vanished before her eyes.

SECRETS OF AN OLD FIREPLACE

When I acquired Saddlers in 1974 my curiosity was aroused by the living-room fireplace. It was an uninteresting brickette and tile affair quite out of keeping with the character of an eighteenth-century cottage. What really attracted my attention was not the ugly little fireplace but the massive thickness of the wall in which it was sited. Could it be, I wondered, that an older, larger fireplace lurked behind?

One afternoon, torch in hand, I stuck my head and shoulders up the flue and the light shone into a brick-lined cavern. I had found an inglenook! Enquiries of a neighbour, whose grandmother had lived in the cottage many years before, confirmed my findings. 'There used to be a big fireplace with little seats either side. You didn't sit in them too long though as 'twere too hot!'

A local builder demolished the modern hideousness to reveal a brick inglenook fireplace – and the little seats – with a chamfered wooden lintel holding up the old chalk, mud and straw wall. Everything was very sooty, dusty and damp and yet fascinating though this discovery was, it faded into insignificance at the sight of some objects tucked away on the right-hand seat.

The 'find' consisted of a pair of child's boots, probably from the 1870s, a woman's boot of the 1890s, and a woman's shoe of the 1930s. The child's boots were interesting because they had no lace holes or obvious means of fastening. In addition, there were the remains of two old leather gaiters, the broken tine of a pitchfork, a trivet or kettle-stand, a modern penknife and pair of pliers, and a small cardboard box.

This box bears the name of Cooke & Kelvey, 'Diamond Merchants, Jewellers, Watch, Clock & Chronometer Makers, Scindia House, Queensway, New Delhi.' How it came to Piddletrenthide can only be conjectured, but the old Dorset Regiment saw much service in India. In the box is an assortment of press-studs and hooks and eyes, many unused and still sewn to their original backing cards, some bearing the legend 'Newey's Finest Hard Steel Wire Extra Japanned Finish.' The style of printing suggests the early part of this century.

All the footwear is in a very poor state, each item being well worn and the leather dirty and brittle. Indeed, the heel of the woman's boot came away while it was being handled. The metal objects are equally poor and are rusty, even the comparatively recent penknife and pliers.

At first I imagined that these objects were merely so much rubbish thrown into the fireplace before it was sealed. However, with the aid of knowledgeable friends and a little research, my first impressions were shown to be very wrong, for it seems that this hoard represents a superstition going back to the Middle Ages and possibly even earlier.

The superstition requires old, worn footwear to be concealed in new or altered dwellings in order to bring good luck to the house. Other items used for the same purpose are iron and bones, and the usual places for concealment are in fireplaces or under thresholds. The superstition does not appear to be confined solely to Dorset – indeed, records exist of similar finds in America; nor have such objects been limited to humble dwellings, for old shoes have been discovered in Tewkesbury Abbey and St John's College, Oxford.

The placing of these items in the fireplace can be compared to another superstition which is Dorset in origin: that of hanging in the chimney a sheep's or bullock's heart stuffed with pins or thorns. The reason for this is that, while doors and chimneys may be barred against witches, the chimney still provides entry to the house. Access can be denied to a witch by the presence of such a heart. The old footwear and iron in the fireplace may have served the dual purpose of deterring witches and bringing good luck.

So much for the superstition, but when and by whom were these objects hidden in Saddlers? In the early 1960s many alterations were made to the cottage by the then owner, who was an architect, and evidently he was responsible for bricking up the old fireplace. Yet this does not explain the age-range of the objects. My neighbour provided a possible answer, for he can recall seeing some old boots in the fireplace when he was a small boy and thinks they may have belonged to his aunt. If so, they could well have occupied their place in the inglenook since before the turn of the century.

When the fireplace was bricked up, were these things treated as useless rubbish, or was someone conscious of the superstition? If the former, why not just throw them away? Again, if the former why the modern penknife and pliers, which could well date from the early 1960s? I like to think that the superstition was still acknowledged within the last two decades and that it was sufficiently strong for someone to add a modern contribution. Perhaps it was all done by local workmen behind the owner's back and without his knowledge. I do not feel that the presence of Cooke & Kelvey's box can be explained as part of the superstition, but one can have many guesses as to how the box came to be hidden.

While I am one of those who happily walk under ladders, I admit to a feeling of distinct unease when the items were taken away from the house to be dated by a friend. There was a sense of relief and security when they were returned a few days later. I know that I shall not readily let them pass out of the cottage again and I wonder if I should not perhaps add another well-worn boot to the collection!

B. K. ROY

ST KATHARINE'S CHAPEL

There is a legend which says that there used to be a secret passage between the Abbey at Cerne and Cat-and-Chapel Hill, the hill connecting Cerne Abbas with Piddletrenthide. On top of the hill is the site of a chapel dedicated to St Katharine, the patron saint of spinsters, and to the chapel went the unmarried ladies of the Piddle Valley, praying to the saint that she would send them a husband:

> Sweet St Katharine send me a husband,
> A good one I pray:
> But arn a one better than narn a one.
> Oh, St Katharine
> Lend me thine aid
> And grant that I never may
> Die an old maid.

Cat-and-Chapel is almost certainly a corruption of St Katharine's Chapel. Another chapel dedicated to the saint, who according to local inhabitants is still carrying out her charitable work as a marriage bureau, is at Abbotsbury. It is not easy to find out if the saint is equally efficacious in the Piddle Valley!

An old farmer, George Tom, who lived near the vicarage, used to ride his horse round the farm day in and day out. One day the horse died and he told his men to dig a hole in the field behind his house and bury it.

'Why bury him with his saddle and bridle on, Guv'nor?' asked Jack Tucker.

'Because when I die,' replied old George, 'I'm going to be buried beside that horse, so that when the day of judgement comes I can get on his back and ride straight to hell!'

Bird Lore, Weather Lore, Country Cures and Potions

THE MAGPIE

The handsome magpie, thieving and predatory, is the object of more superstition in the Valley than any other bird, perhaps because it shows little fear of man and often crosses his path in its slow, looping flight; also because it is a well-known robber, sometimes even venturing through a window to steal a ring or other glittering trinket which attracts it.

Many villagers still say: 'Good morning, Mr Magpie, how are you today?' and raise their hat respectfully when they see one. Others will spit over their shoulder or cross themselves to ensure that they will not be dogged by ill luck for the rest of the day. It is not unknown for a dweller in the Valley, setting out on a journey, to turn back if he sees a magpie on the way. 'Better safe than sorry,' he will say.

There is a rhyme about magpies which is still often quoted:

> One for sorrow,
> Two for joy,
> Three for a girl,
> Four for a boy,
> Five for silver,
> Six for gold,
> Seven for a secret that's never been told.

Fortunately, magpies are faithful creatures, rarely apart from their mates, and so a single specimen 'for sorrow' is unusual and 'two for joy' the common sight. They are gregarious birds, occasionally seen in flocks of as many as thirty, although the verse allows for only seven, and the spring congregation of magpies, when pairs as well as single birds gather together for display and courtship, is a sight to delight the eye of any ornithologist.

THE ROBIN

A robin tapping at a window pane is a sign that there will shortly be a death in the house.

WEATHER LORE

Most Valley farmers listen to the radio weather forecast, but only to reinforce what they have already learned from long-respected signs and portents, for instance:

If the 'whistling plover' is heard in the fields it is a sign that the fine weather will break and a storm is brewing. The 'whistling plover', as it is known in the Valley, is not a plover at all but the curlew.

While the cherry trees in the garden of Piddlehinton Manor House are in flower the weather will be rough. As soon as the blossom falls it will become fine.

If snow continues to hang about the fields and hedges after a thaw, Piddle Valley people say 'it is waiting for more to come.' Some people claim that they can actually smell the coming of snow. Those who are not able to do this can still forecast frost and snow by the behaviour of the birds. If they are seen picking up scraps of wool and hair, it means that they are looking for cosy bedding. They poke the scraps into wall cracks, hedges and nest boxes, and huddle in the 'blankets' to keep warm. When frost is forecast, Lois Wright always puts out hair combings and snippets of cotton wool and they are gratefully accepted. She also has permanent nest boxes nailed up in the porch of her house in Piddletrenthide and on more than one occasion has seen as many as twenty-four birds – chiefly tits and sparrows – come out of a box after a particularly chilly night.

When rooks, wheeling about the sky in huge flocks, suddenly swoop in unison towards the ground, it is a forecast of stormy weather. This is known in the Valley as 'flying breakneck'. Cocks crowing at any time of the day are a sign of rain to come, and a blackbird whistling presages a thunderstorm.

But if cattle are seen feeding at the top of a hill during a rainstorm, the weather will soon clear.

LOVE CHARMS AND POTIONS

The Piddle Valley has many willow trees. To awaken ardour, steep willow seeds in spring water, give it to your beloved to drink and your love will be returned.

The bed sheets of lovers should be scented with marjoram to arouse desire. (When Venus carried off Adonis she laid him on a bed of this fragrant herb.)

A sprig of verbena tucked into the pillow is also reckoned to be efficacious.

CHARMING WARTS

Some country doctors advise their patients to visit a local wart charmer to have their warts removed rather than submit to the unpleasant treatment of having them burnt off.

One Valley method is for the charmer to rub the wart with the pod of a broad bean. The pod is then buried in the garden and when it rots the wart will fall off. This is a proven success.

Another way is to rub the wart with the sap of an elder twig in springtime.

A CURE FOR THE WHOOPING COUGH

Catch a shrew-mouse. Bore a hole in the trunk of an ash tree, put in the shrew and plug the hole with clay. When the entombed shrew dies, the whooping cough will be cured.

There is a field some way beyond Piddlehinton known as

Shear Ashes, which used to have a gigantic ash tree in the centre of it. The name is probably a corruption of 'Shrew's Ash' and may have been another place where this somewhat gruesome cure was practised.

A CURE FOR THE TOOTHACHE

Mrs Hicks was a teacher in Piddletrenthide School from 1889 to 1924. Her son Harry vividly remembers this recipe: set fire to a bit of rag, blow out the flame and let it smoulder. Then block the nostril on the opposite side to the aching tooth and sniff the smoke up the nose. It is a certain cure.

AN EYE LOTION

Mrs Hicks also had a cure for sore eyes. She used to send Harry up to Kingrove to pick Eyebright, with its white and purple flowers. This she would hang up in the larder to dry and then take off a few sprigs, put them in a cup and pour boiling water over them. When cool, the lotion was used to bathe the eyes.

NANNY BAKER'S COUNTRY CURES

For a cough make a syrup of onion and brown sugar. Put a layer of onion in a small basin, cover this with brown sugar, do this two or three times, place a saucer on top and leave overnight. Drink a dessertspoonful three or four times a day.

For chest troubles pick fresh garlic leaves and wear like 'inside socks' in your shoes. This penetrates the system. When the leaves dry up, pick fresh ones.

For healing septic places, poultice with marshmallow or dandelion leaves.

COUNTRY CURES FOR ANIMALS

Many farmers still practise their own folk remedies on sick animals. As veterinary surgeon F. K. Fletcher says, they will try all the old cures first, such as hanging a garland of wild thyme round the neck of a sick cow. If those fail, as a last resort they will call in the vet.

Mr Fletcher and his colleague, veterinary surgeon Colin Grist of Piddlehinton, have noted the following remedies still used round the Valley:

Lameness in cattle: the sod where the foot has trodden is cut out and thrown into a blackthorn bush.

Preventing abortion in cattle: (a) run a goat with the herd; (b) the aborted foetus is flung into an elder bush.

Farrowing problems in the sow: the animal is given a drink of dandelion tea.

Removal of warts: apply the juice of the sun spurge to the wart.

To ensure a clean birth: raspberry-leaf tea is given at the first sign of the birth.

TELLING THE BEES

It is still the custom for bee-keepers to inform their bees if there is a death or a marriage in the family. They go down the garden to the hive, tap on it and tell the inmates: 'Granfer has died – he has gone on now,' or, 'Our Mary is to be wed tomorrow.' This is to keep the bees happy and to prevent them from forsaking the hive.

George Jakeman recalls the time when he used to help bee-keeper Lady Jackson take off her honey. Lady Jackson was the wife of General Sir Henry Jackson, one of Piddletrenthide's most famous residents. After she died, Mr Jakeman learned that she had wished him to have her bees and so he took charge of them. Within three months, however, they had all died or deserted the hive. Puzzled, he mentioned it to Nellie Hollands, the General's housekeeper.

'Did you tell the bees of Lady Jackson's death?' asked Nellie.

Mr Jakeman confessed that he had omitted to do so.

'That is why the bees have gone,' he was told.

PIDDLE VALLEY SAYINGS

Cuckoo Corn

Corn sown after 7 April is known in the Valley as 'cuckoo corn' because you can often hear the cuckoo making its familiar call during the time of sowing. It is a pejorative term: late sowing invariably means a poor harvest.

'The man who buys keep is a fool and the man who sells keep is a fool.'

The interpretation of this is: if a farmer has to buy keep he has too many cattle; if he has some to sell he has too few.

If you see the sun shining through the bare branches of an apple tree on Christmas Day it forecasts a fine summer and a good crop of apples.

The River Piddle

The Piddle rises in the village of Alton St Pancras. Most people look for its source in a gravelly area about half a mile west of the church and just above a copse known as Soggy Wood. Others claim that the spring is a few hundred yards north, near Holcombe Dairy Farm. Certainly a little stream does rise from there and flows under a succession of narrow bridges that lead to the houses and cottages lining the main street. But as this stream diminishes to a trickle and sometimes dries up altogether in time of drought, the other source seems more likely. Rivers, of course, can have more than one source; another tributary comes down the hills from Plush to join the main stream near Piddletrenthide Manor House, and there are also seven springs at Morning Well, just beyond Piddletrenthide Church, which help to augment the flow.

A few yards west of Soggy Wood is Rake Bottom, a flat area of flint and gravel embroidered with the white flowers of wild watercress. Here you can actually see the springs bubbling up and disturbing the sand. It is said that there are twenty-one of them. Beyond is a dry river valley which suggests that the water table has dropped at some time, with the result that the Piddle springs up at the present source.

From there it flows through Soggy Wood, which is composed of ivy-clad ash trees, hawthorn and sycamore. There is, too, horse chestnut, willow and typha, an aquatic plant of the reed-mace family. Poplars were planted in the 1940s by the then Lord of the Manor, Col. F. P. Saunders. Most of them have now been cut down, but the copse remains a haven for wild life, and a number of mallards, particularly, have made it their home.

There was not always a wood here, however. At some time in the past a dam was built to create a boating lake, but unfortunately this was breached in 1909 after a severe frost followed by flood. Warning of the impending inundation was brought to the villagers of Piddletrenthide by a passing carter who urged his horse down the Valley at a speed which the poor old horse must have felt was unwarranted! The gap in the stonework of the dam can still be clearly seen. In fact, today the river flows through it in a noisy little waterfall, and then widens into placid gravelly shallows. It continues through a field which may once have been a water meadow but has now been channelled into a straight course with man-made banks on either side. Halfway along it spreads out into a pond known as the Monks' Bathing Pool, although what monks bathed there – if indeed any did – remains a mystery. Beyond the pool the river enters a culvert and goes underground, reappearing along the north side of the church, swerving northwards by Austral Farm and then reaching the main road, where it turns south and makes its way across fields and meadows to Piddletrenthide and Piddlehinton.

From its source at Alton St Pancras to the mouth in Poole Harbour is a distance of twenty miles, and on its way the Piddle passes through a number of villages which take their names from the river: Piddletrenthide, Piddlehinton, Puddletown, Tolpuddle, Affpuddle, Briantspuddle and Turners Puddle. Most of the original 'piddles' have become 'puddles', a change almost certainly due to Victorian prudery, some say to the prudery of no less a person than Queen Victoria herself! There is still no complete uniformity of name on maps and in local newspapers.

Eventually the river reaches Wareham, where it once formed the northern defences of that Anglo-Saxon town while the River Frome constituted the southern boundary, and from there both rivers find their way down into the estuary at Poole.

In the Valley, five mills once used the River Piddle to drive their wheels: Alton Mill, Church Mill, Manor Mill, Lackington Mill and Piddlehinton Mill, all of which are mentioned in the Domesday Book. Those at Alton, Piddletrenthide Manor and Piddlehinton belonged to the manor house in their respective villages and to them the tenants of the manor were obliged to bring their grist, the miller being entitled to a percentage of all the corn ground. It was a further obligation on the tenants to spend the Thursday in Whitsun week cleaning and scouring the mill pond.

The mills gradually fell into disuse. The one at Piddlehinton was worked as recently as 1930, operating then as a saw mill. It has the distinction of having had at one time a female miller, Mrs Caroline Clarke in 1890. Lackington or Lower Tything Mill ceased work about two years earlier and Church Mill about the same time. Lackington Mill was fed by a leat, or channel, which left the river at Nine Hole Hatch. This name indicates the flow that had to be maintained in the river itself whatever the volume needed to drive the mill. The requirement, legally enforcible, was one reason why in some cases a mill pond was constructed, so that a small flow of water could be collected overnight or between workings and drawn upon when needed. The mill wheel, as in other mills, could also be coupled to cider-making machinery.

At Austral Farm, Alton St Pancras, the river was at one time diverted near the source at Rake Bottom, the water being conveyed by a very ingenious system to drive a wheel which powered machines such as a chaff cutter, a cake cracker and an oat bruiser. In due course the water power was superseded by steam, then by a stationary petrol engine, by a tractor and finally by electricity. Each system in turn played its part in helping to prepare food for the livestock.

The river was also used in the past for flooding the fields and so forming water meadows which helped to enrich the pasture for sheep and cattle. This practice, dating from at least the early seventeenth century, meant that the stream could be diverted from its natural path to a higher level and made to overflow so that a thin blanket of running water covered the meadows, returning eventually to the river. This 'floating' or 'drowning' was carried on intermittently from early October until Lady Day (25 March). After the first flooding sheep would be folded on the grass, usually

between February and May, and then after a second flooding the ground would be dried and cattle grazed in July, August and September. Today, improved grass strains and modern fertilizers have done away with the need for flooding to promote the early growth of grass.

In spite of the proximity of houses and people along some reaches of the river, there is still an abundance of wild life. Otters are no longer seen, but the breathtaking blue and gold flash of a kingfisher can occasionally be glimpsed; sadly, one was caught and killed by a Lackington cat not so long ago. Moorhens are fairly common, and a pair brought up their family last year on the stretch bertween Sun Lane and Swan Lane. Grey herons flap lazily up and down searching for fish; one regular visitor patrols the river most mornings on the look-out for his breakfast. During one of the recurrent winter freezes, it so happened that David Wightman was dredging the bed of the stream with his river digger. The scoop threw up loads of mud on to the bank and the mud was alive with eels. It was so cold that the mud began to freeze as it landed. That same foraging heron must have seen the harvest and taken word back to the heronry in near-by Puddletown Forest, for soon the bank was a feeding ground for an army of herons, all finding great difficulty in disentangling their lunch from the freezing mud. The next day the remaining eels were frozen stiff, but the herons would not give up. They tugged at their prey, now contorted into all sorts of queer shapes, banged them on the mud and eventually swallowed what must have been an extremely cold meal.

The Piddle is not always the placid, gentle stream, lined with comfrey and wild forget-me-not and providing a shelter for bird, fish and mammal, that is seen by the summer visitor. Sometimes in winter, when wind and rain combine into a wild storm, it overflows its banks. Streams of rainwater cascading down the hills from Plush augment the flood. The culverts and drains taking the excess water cannot cope and the main road becomes a raging torrent. Householders are not safe, even with their doors sandbagged, and in 1979 it happened twice in seven months that the water invaded their homes and their carpets and furniture were ruined.

Hey diddle, hey diddle, hey diddle
I live on the banks of the Piddle,
But if it should flood
There is no doubt I should
Be in piddle right up to my middle.

Badger Watching

A grey squirrel returning to its drey discovers my hiding-place, ten feet up in the fork of an old beech tree. Thirty feet away is a large hole in the ground, fronted by an enormous mound of earth. I am trying to watch badgers, but the squirrel has other ideas. Chattering with suspicion and looking at me first from the right and then from the left, it flicks its tail in agitation. Since I don't move, it eventually decides that I'm not dangerous and moves off through the top branches. The sun sets early behind the chalk hills that rim this deep valley and it is getting quite dark. A buzzard finishes its final sweep over a near-by field and returns to its nest in an old Scots Pine, while the woodland birds make their final vocal arrangements for the evening. The chiff-chaffs finished long ago, leaving a robin to its tentative and self-absorbed solo. Blackbirds are fussily ticking away the daylight and a rather pompous cock pheasant seems to be trying to ward off dusk with its raucous yells. All the time there has been an inconspicuous background trill that at last has the stage for a few minutes as a grasshopper warbler, as busy as a sewing machine, stitches the ends of the day together. A nightingale starts up: it must be a quarter of a mile away, but you can't mistake it in the creeping gloom.

Something is moving down the slope, slowly and care-fully pushing between the hazel bushes. It is a roe deer hind making her way to the bottom of the wood, where she can feed on a field of grass made lush by the benefit of modern fertilizers. She makes painfully slow progress, stopping every now and again to nibble the leaves from bushes whose details I can scarcely make out in the gathering dark, picking her way with great delicacy: a contrast to the crunching of leaves and snapping of twigs that accompanied my arrival in the wood. With what I consider to be infinite slowness I pick up my binoculars, but she catches the movement, and with a clicking of heels and a series of jumps like a springbok's she is off up the slope.

A grey silence settles over the wood. My eyes are straining to detect any movement at the entrance to the badgers' sett. Suddenly a sound as loud as that of a kangaroo hopping through the leaves makes me swing my head round. I can't see anything, but the sound tells me that a wood mouse has left its hole and is after breakfast. There is a sudden movement at the sett entrance and my heart beats faster, but it is only a rabbit sharing the same front door though a different bedroom. Fifty feet away up the hill and higher than my seat, a rapid trot announces the passage of a vixen intent on catching food for her three cubs waiting in a disused badger sett half a mile away in the side of the next valley.

I close my eyes, to quell the impatience that memory and anticipation force upon me. Suddenly from behind there is the sound of vigorous scratching. The old boar has emerged from a different entrance. He must have been standing there quietly for some time, scenting the air with flared nostrils, before he decided that all was well and he could settle to the delicious business of grooming his long coarse hair. This is a good sign: when badgers scratch you may be sure that they are not worried. I relax again and wonder what to do about the midges that are crawling over my eyelids. Just as I start to raise my gloved hand to smear them away, three small shapes burst from the hole in front of me: this year's cubs intent on exploring their surroundings. Suddenly one starts a game of tag by biting its brother's bottom, and they are off on a rampaging and rumbustious game that flattens several square yards of bluebells. Their mother appears at the sett entrance and calls with a low, throaty, purring growl. They rush to her and there are a few moments of the ritual grooming and the general frivolous rough-housing that passes for family togetherness in badgers. During this, they set scent on each other from their under-tail glands. It is the family mixture of smells that they all carry which acts as an identity card in the dark.

Now it is time for the serious business of feeding, and the sow leads her cubs down one of their well-worn paths and out on to the green pasture below the wood. The night is damp and the earthworms are lying out of their burrows with only their tails to anchor them. The badger's major food is the earthworm, and the sow has only to lead the cubs to this favourite feeding ground and they are off on a harvest of succulent delights, perfecting the instinctive craft of extracting the resisting worms from their burrows.

I am left with the task of moving from my tree with the minimum of noise and creep off to the road, knowing that the badgers will probably not return until dawn.

A car-flattened hedgehog is such a common sight that we fear for the survival of the species. In our valley badgers commonly meet their death in the same violent way. Many villagers have seen more dead badgers than live ones and the majority of people living here have never seen a live badger at all. It is the badger's habit of following traditional foot-paths across roads with ever-increasing traffic which brings the downfall of so many. However, they continue to survive in such numbers that a determined badger-watcher can happily spend an evening watching these splendid animals. With patience and a quickly acquired skill you find that watching badgers is easier than watching any other British mammal. Not that our valley badgers are tamer than others. Far from it. They are so disturbed by the earth-stoppers of the local hunt that they are more wary than in many other areas. Yet it is a popular place for badgers: there are many steep hills and banks ideal for tunnelling into. Some banks are natural, others are the lynchets resulting from strip cultivation. The setts are either near the edge of a wood or in a hedgerow. The badgers prefer old hedges, the Anglo-Saxon estate boundaries, rather than the plain quickthorn hedges of nineteenth-century enclosure. There is even a sett in the great unfinished rampart of our local iron age fort. Everywhere the setts are in chalk, with a great pile of pale soil and flints outside, surrounded by nettles and elder-bushes. From one side of Plush Valley on an early summer day you can pick out the badger setts on the other side, marked as they are by white splashes of either chalk or elderflower.

Even in our most severe winters the badgers don't hibernate, and after a fall of snow you can visit the setts and follow the owners' trails across country for many miles. Of course there is little food for them then, and so their body chemistry slows right down to allow them to exist on the rich layers of body fat built up by their autumn foraging. In December the sun passes its lowest point in the sky. Inside the sow's body the eggs fertilized many months before lie dormant. As the sun begins to climb the sky again an astonishing thing happens: the dormant eggs suddenly start to grow. Some time in the middle of February the cubs are born with three whole seasons before them in which to savour the delights of the Piddle Valley before themselves retiring to endure the next solstice.

MALCOLM HOWELL

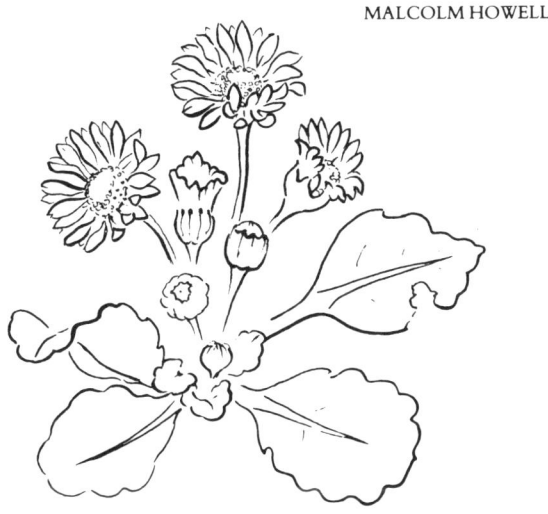

The Weasel

Sinuous ripple through the pasture flowing,
Limbless progression as of barley blowing,
The wave abruptly ceased.
He paused erect, buff coat and white front showing:
Fabulous serpent-beast!

He conned the field with eye of black japan
And smiling ivory to hunt began,
Terror of mouse and vole!
Long, lithe, liquid, silently he ran:
Natural pest control!

GEORGE DARWALL

A Valley of Flowers

In the spring the Piddle Valley is a valley of snowdrops.
They grow wild along the hedgerows and at Snowdrop
Corner, where the road makes a wide, sweeping turn to
Waterston Ridge, they are as thick beneath the trees as drifts
of snow. Primroses are scarcer. A few can be seen peeping
shyly from the south-facing banks and hedges, but you have
to go to Alton St Pancras and more especially to Plush to see
more of them. The name 'primrose' means 'first flower',
but the lesser celandines which everywhere cover the fields
with yellow stars are usually earlier. A little later, a few
precious areas of pasture are studded with cowslips, once
common but now so rare that a national Sunday newspaper
recently held a survey to discover how many still existed
in the whole of Britain. Rare they may be, but at
Plush and White Lackington, on slopes too steep for
the plough, they still flower in profusion until grazed
by the cattle, and happily appear year after year.
Occasionally in Plush there can be found another real
treasure, the oxlip, a hybrid of the primrose family and
even more handsome with its umbrella of yellow flowers.

Daffodils and narcissus grow along the verges, not
the rare wild variety but garden flowers that
have either been

planted by community-conscious villagers or have natura-
lized themselves from discarded bulbs, to delight the eye of
the passer-by. The earliest spring flowers seem almost without exception to be white or bright yellow, perhaps in order
the more successfully to entice reluctant insects to brave the
cold winds in their search for nectar. But a little later on
yellow gives way to blue and there are bluebells, wild
hyacinths, growing in the hedges and copses in scattered
clumps, although they do not form the miraculous blue
haze which turns Batcombe Wood a few miles away into a
world of enchantment and carpets the brackeny slopes
around Hardy's Monument above Martinstown. A denser
carpet of blue is formed in the Valley by the germander
speedwell, which covers the ground everywhere and seems
especially to thrive on molehills. On the chalky hills of
Plush there are also smaller but no less striking rich blue
patches of the chalk milkwort, not found lower down in
Piddletrenthide.

At the end of spring the lanes are lined with cow parsley,
known in Dorset as 'gypsy's lace', so that you drive through
avenues of thick foaming cream interspersed with the bright
pink flowers of the red campion, and as spring drifts into
summer white and pink dog roses sprawl in profusion
across the hedges, filling the air with their fragrance. Along
the banks of the Piddle is comfrey, both the pink-and-blue
variety and the white, a herb thought from early times to
have great medicinal powers. In his Herbal, the sixteenth-
century herbalist John Gerard says: '. . . the slimie substance
of the roote made in a posset of ale, and given to drinke
against the paine in the backe, gotten by an violent motion,
as wrestling or over much use of women, doth in fower or
five daies perfectly cure the same.' We do not know if
anyone in the Valley has tried it for back ache, but certainly
the leaves make a useful vegetable if boiled like spinach and
well seasoned with salt and pepper. The hairiness of their
undersides entirely disappears in the cooking.

By the riverside, too, grows an occasional butterbur,
with the largest leaves of any British wild plant, not particularly beautiful to look at but a rare treat for the amateur
botanist.

In the copses and coverts there are innumerable wild arums, known by so many different names: dead men's fingers, because of the colour of the apex and the putrid smell which attracts flies and other insects; Jack-in-the-pulpit, the flower being supposedly like a parson in his purple cassock appearing above the pulpit rail to preach his sermon; cuckoo pint, from the belief that cuckoos drank the liquid that collected in the base; and wake robin because of the scarlet fruits that emerge like a red resurrection from the withered sheath. Although the berries are poisonous and should be avoided at all costs, the roots when cooked and pounded in a mortar become entirely harmless; they were once used as a form of flour or arrowroot under the name of Portland sago, a considerable trade in the commodity being carried out on the Isle of Portland.

Deeper in the woods and along shaded hedgerows you can smell ransoms, a form of wild garlic whose shining green leaves, looking very much like those of the lily-of-the-valley, can be chopped and used as mild garlic flavouring.

At this time the chalk hillsides of Plush produce many botanical treasures: the curious reddish-brown globular heads of the salad burnet and the rare bee orchid which so strikingly resembles the insect from which it takes its name. Sometimes only six, sometimes a dozen or more, may be grouped in a small area but, curiously, a different area each year, although perhaps less than a hundred yards away from the previous one. The explanation is probably not that the bee orchid 'travels' but that the plants have a rest period of several years before flowering anew. Another member of the orchid family is the twayblade, so called from its single pair of leaves ('two bladed'), with a spike of greenish-yellow flowers standing up tall and erect from the turf of shady pasturelands. As the bee orchid and the twayblade fade – and their blooms last all to short a time – the south-facing slopes are suddenly covered with the golden rock rose and the eyebright with its purple and white lip. There are also the tiny pink flowers, delicately almond-scented, of the aquinancy wort. It is a reputed cure for quinsy; hence its curious name.

Summer finds the verges lining the lanes and droves thick with pale lilac scabious, one of the Valley's commonest summer flowers, and the ubiquitous rosebay willow herb, so familiar in city waste-lands, whose pods, when they burst, fill the air with fluffy white seedheads like drifting snow. The banks are bright with sweet-scented bedstraw, both the white and yellow varieties. Lady's bedstraw, with its profusion of yellow flowers, is probably so called because it was once used by aristocratic ladies to stuff their mattresses. No doubt the fragrance had a soporific effect! It is also known as cheese-rennet, having been employed in the past to curdle milk in cheese-making and to give the cheeses their rich golden colour.

At this time of the year the fields are golden with ragwort, unloved by the farmer because of its toxic effect on his cattle. Although harmless when alive because it is too sour for the cows to eat, the plant becomes palatable when dead and can have dire consequences. On the chalk downs are the pale yellow hawkweeds, members of the dandelion family, the bold purple heads of the knapweed and the narrow, pale-violet trumpets of the chalk field gentian. There is the Carline thistle, closely related to the true thistles, so called from the legend which tells of an angel who gave the root to the Emperor Charlemagne (Carolus or Karl) as a remedy against the plague. Members of the campanula family thrive on the chalk: the dainty harebell and, much rarer but still fairly plentiful on the hillsides of Plush, the low-lying purple-blue clustered bellflower.

Now it is autumn and the hedgerows are heavy with fruit. In summer the elder bushes, perhaps the most common of all flowering trees in the Valley apart from the hawthorn or may, yielded up their clotted-cream flowers for elderflower champagne; in autumn the black fruits are used for the making of delicious jam and wine. Scarlet rose hips are picked for jam and syrup, and the blackthorn, which covered the hedges with white foam in early spring, now provides sloes for that most delectable of all liqueurs, sloe gin. Blackberries are everywhere for the picking, although sadly not as many as there used to be with the disappearance of many hedges but they must not be gathered after 11 October (Michaelmas Day in the Old Calendar). On that day Satan was cast out from Heaven and fell into a blackberry bush, and ever since he has come up from below on the same day to curse the blackberries. Thereafter they are not fit to eat, tasting soft and acrid and often covered with 'cuckoo spit'! There are also the crimson berries of the hawthorn, luscious-looking with their heavy heads but eaten only by the birds.

Among the brambles twines the wild clematis, traveller's joy, which bears insignificant greenish-white flowers in the spring but is now a mass of feathery fruits known as old man's beard for obvious reasons, and the green-and-orange glaucous fruits of the bryony, with its rope-like twisted stems. Colour is everywhere: crimson and scarlet, orange and bright green, purple and black. Often the fruits cling on until December, and then in a month or two the snowdrops begin to poke their green spears through the frozen earth and the whole flower cycle begins all over again.

ERIC MURRELL & MURIEL PIKE

'The Voices of Children . . .'

THE RIVER

'I like living in the Piddle Valley because there is a river and you can catch fish . . .' (Tracey Downton, 8).

'I love to listen to the water lapping and see redthroats and bullheads in the clear water' (Emily Cooper).

'It is nice and cool for me to waggle my feet in' (Kerry Dixon, 7½).

'There is a river running through the Valley which goes to Poole Harbour' (Andrew Hawker, (9½).

'The river is infested with minnows, bullheads and eels. It's got a tributary leading into it called "Rushing Torrent" – well, that's what I call it. It was man-made and its purpose is to drain the fields. Rushing Torrent is a lovely little stream with splashing waterfalls which spray the water out like fast-moving crystals' (Justin Waddy, 11).

'The best thing I like about the country is walking in the fields and listening to the water as it flows over the pebbles' (Sarah Marsh).

'There is a very long river that you can go paddling in' (Jillian Lambert, 10).

'I love playing with the river' (Joanne Hawker, 5).

'One day our school went down by the stream. I heard the waterfall and the bees buzzing among the reeds' (Michelle Raymond).

'In the summer I sit and read down by Piddle River. I sit on a large root and hear the song thrush sing' (Andrea Dixon, 9).

'In the winter the mist hangs over the water, while snow-covered trees shake in the wind' (Ben Newbery, 9).

LIFE ON THE FARM

'I can help on the farm because my Dad works there. You can hear the cows going to be milked and tractors going up and down the road' (Andrew Hawker).

'When harvesting time comes my friend and I help the farmer to gather the corn in. The combine consumes the corn like a huge snarling monster. In summer I help to collect the bales' (Barry Gear).

'In the morning you can hear the cows going down to the dairy to be milked' (Rebecca Buchan, 8).

'I like watching the tractors' (Michael Buchan, 5).

'In mid-July you can bale the hay and its smell is lovely' (Andrea Dixon).

'Sometimes some sheep or calves come through the village and the traffic is held up. The shepherd walks in front closing gates whilst the sheepdogs follow' (Lois Spiller).

'We go and collect the eggs in a barn. The hens lay their eggs all over the place in the hay and we have to search for them. Then we go and fetch the cows from the fields so that the farmer can milk them' (Richard Szarat).

'Sometimes I go shooting rabbits with my Daddy and my sister. One night we took some string to tie the rabbits on so that I wouldn't have to carry them in my hand' (Lavinia).

'Sometimes I go rabbiting with my uncle. We use ferrets to get the rabbits out. We put nets over the holes. We sometimes have to dig the ferret out' (David Osgood).

COUNTRY CREATURES

'One day we saw a squirrel climbing a tree' (Diane Legg).

'In spring I listen for the cuckoo and watch the martins flying in the sky. They sit on the wires twittering' (Michelle Raymond).

'I like watching the hunt go by' (Daniel Newbery, 6).

'There were two foxes in the garden . . .'

'Every morning at seven the blackbird comes on our washing line. In springtime the martins live under the eaves of our house' (Diane Legg).

'In the morning you can hear the pigeons' (Lucy Scragg, 8).

'Sometimes when you go up the main road you see deer in the fields on each side' (Andrea Dixon).

'Especially I love to go down to the copse to listen to the cuckoo and gather firewood for my Mum' (Emily Cooper).

THE VILLAGE

'The old church staring out in the deep blue sky' (Billy Meehan, 10).

'The hills are good for go-cart races' (James Ingleton, 10).

'Ice dangling from the frosted thatch . . .' (Heather Cousins).

'Houses made out of brick, flint and cob' (Rachel Downes, 9).

'I like living in the Piddle Valley because it is nice and peaceful' (Andrew Jones, 6).

'The people are friendly' (Nicholas Andrew, 9).

'Every Sunday the church bells are ringing' (Jillian Lambert).

'It's got a good community spirit. When the heavy snow-fall came in February, 1978, people were giving out milk and everybody was working hard to clear the roads with snowploughs' (Stephen Green, 12).

'People walking by the green and brown river; the fifteenth-century church; wheat and barley growing in the fields; the nineteenth-century school with its Westminster Abbey gates; the cold winter and the hot summer; the friendly people; the hall plates reminding us of the men who died in the war; the brick and flint houses with their tiled and thatched roofs; and the chalk downs' (Derick Abbott, 9).

'There's not much in this little Valley but enough to keep me jolly and happy' (Jayne West, 11½).

THE WOOD IN WINTER

I walk alone in the solitude of the lonely wood. To my joy it is snowing. The flakes are like tiny angels falling from heaven to celebrate the approach of Christmas Day. Ahead lies a long white expanse of smooth, untrodden snow. I feel guilty when my foot comes down and invades this sea of angels. There is no sound except for the glistening, melancholy song of the Christmas bird, or robin as it is more usually called.

The big oak looks all forlorn as its majestic branches spiral up to the sky. A late leaf falls, twisting and turning with the icy wind, and lands gracefully on the bed of snow. The hawthorn's red berries are being plucked off by the ever-hungry Scandinavian invaders, the fieldfares and redwings. Their chatter cuts like a razor through the icy stillness. The groan of the compressed snow under my feet attracts the inquisitive robin; it pecks round my feet for even a tiny morsel of food but none is found. I feel sorry for it, so I delve into my pockets with salmon-pink hands and pull out a sandwich. The pain of hunger kills the sense of fear in the tiny bird as it pecks at the sandwich. When it has had enough it flies to the big oak tree and pours out a flowing song in gratitude for my gesture.

Along the edge of the narrow track is a whole colonnade of tall, sentry-like beeches. The snow glistens like crystal on their branches as I walk past. They seem to be watching my every move with hidden, watchful eyes. I now approach the river. It is a beautiful sight as it twists and turns to evade the soldier beeches. It makes a lovely tinkling sound and the tiny angels dissolve into nothingness as they hit it.

The angels stop falling out of the sky as quickly and mysteriously as they started and to my dismay a bright sun comes out. Its sharp, straight rays shoot between the trees and start to melt the sea of angels. A fall of tiny droplets of melted snow pours out of the trees, like the tears of the angels as they slowly disappear into oblivion.

The resident buzzard slowly with long-drawn wing beats pulls up to a halt at the topmost branch of the king of trees, after a hard day's search for food over the gently curved white valleys. It mews to its mate, who joins it on the tall, gnarled, weatherworn branch of the mighty oak.

The day passes quickly at this time of the year and soon the pink, fluorescent sun dips down under the other side of the valley. The gods of the wind start to play with each other by sending howling, icy gales into the wood. The screech-owl is nervous; it hurls a lordly, high-pitched scream down the peaceful wood in defiance of the gods of the wind and then sets off hunting, its delicately-made wings brushing past my face as it silently moves off for the kill. I see a deer; it is a well-antlered stag silhouetted against the pale moonlight down the path.

I move off home now, back down the snow blanket of a path. To my mind, the wood is more magnificent than any human invention. It is the unspoiled mark of Mother Nature laid down on earth for all to enjoy. Tomorrow I will return to celebrate Christmas Day with my friends the robin, the fieldfares, the redwings and the king of the wood, the majestic oak.

JULIAN EDEN (aged 15)

Music in the
Valley

It is not altogether inappropriate to recall Thomas Hardy's descriptions of the village choirs of his day, making music in the church, because the four churches of the Piddle Valley continue to provide the motive and the opportunity for much of the music-making in this rural community. Although no one village can support a full choir of men's and boys' voices, there is an organ in each church and enough organists to ensure that the services and concerts can be conducted in a proper manner. Before the war there was a splendid mixed choir in Piddletrenthide, and in recent years a brave attempt has been made to bring mixed voices together again to mark the special festivals of the church's year: Christmas, Easter and Harvest. The choir is steadily growing in numbers, although it is dependent on outside help for the men's voices. It aims to provide a small addition to the regular services in the form of hymns and carols for all seasons, specially arranged to suit its strengths and weaknesses. Some works have even had their first performance in the Valley, for one of the organists, Jill Howell, is also a composer. Two of her compositions, a Harvest Thanksgiving Hymn, with words by a sixteenth-century poet, and the Piddle Valley Stomp are published here for the first time.

The Valley is also becoming known for its handbell ringing. A set of Dutch handbells provides a different sort of music at services and other celebrations, weddings, concerts and so on. The bells run from middle C upwards through two chromatic octaves. They require delicate handling but no previous musical training, and a regular team of six has developed quite an extensive repertoire of familiar and not-so-familiar airs.

As for church bells, Piddletrenthide and Piddlehinton each have a splendid peal which adds to the traditional atmosphere of church festivals. Many of the ringers have been performing for several years, but newcomers can sometimes be prevailed upon to try their hand at what is a difficult, skilled but very rewarding craft.

MARGARET TURNER

At the beginning of this century, H. E. D. Hammond and his brother toured Dorset on their bicycles, visiting singers in towns and villages all over the county and writing down the songs they sang. The only ones from the Piddle Valley were contributed by a certain G. Dowden of White Lackington; they are entitled 'William of the Waggon Train' and 'My Rose in June'. They are reproduced by kind permission of Miss Biddie Kindersley, a frequent visitor to her brother who lives in Piddletrenthide, and the English Folk Dance and Song Society.

The waggon train to which William has been drafted is, of course, the collection of horse-drawn vehicles used to carry supplies of food and ammunition to the advancing English army in the Peninsular War of 1808. Both songs are addressed to a loved one, but while the first is a song of farewell the second is a lyrical expression of affection, a kind of posy of spring and summer flowers.

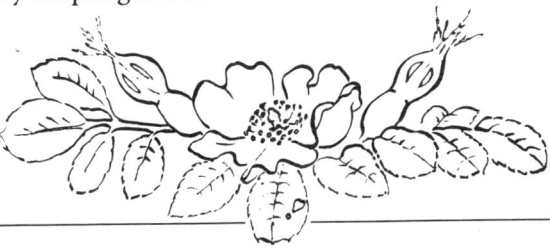

'PLEASURE IT IS': HARVEST THANKSGIVING
HYMN

PIDDLE VALLEY STOMP

TWO PIDDLE VALLEY FOLK SONGS

William of the Waggon Train

One love-ly morn-ing as I was a-walk-ing In the mer-ry month of May, Oh a smart young pair all a-lone was a-talking. I o-ver-heard what they did say. One ap-peared-a love-ly maid-en Seem-ing-ly in grief and pain, And the oth-er he was a gay young sol-dier, A Ser-geant in the Wag-gon Train.

My Rose in June

O my love I will cut down my sweet myrt-le tree. For to build up a cot-tage for Sal-ly and me, So let it be ear-ly, late or soon, I will en-joy my rose in June. Cow-slips make the- etc.

ELLEN TREVETT'S SONG

Mrs Ellen Trevett of Piddlehinton used to sing this song to her daughter, Cissie, now Mrs George Hansford. Although she is now seventy-seven years old, Mrs Hansford remembers every word:

> My father he died and I can't tell you how;
> He gave me six horses to follow the plough.
>> With me wing wang wobble-o,
>> Jack's in saddle-o,
>> Blowsy boys and bubble-o,
>> Under the broom.
>
> I sold the six horses and bought me a cow,
> I then made my fortune but didn't know how.
>> With me wing wang . . . .
>
> I sold me the cow and bought me a calf,
> I then made my fortune but lost my best half.
>> With me wing wang . . . .
>
> I sold me the calf and bought me a cat,
> And all she could do was sit on the mat.
>> With me wing wang . . . .
>
> I sold me the cat and bought me a mouse,
> Whose tail caught on fire and burnt down the house.
>> With me wing wang wobble-o,
>> Jack's in saddle-o,
>> Blowsy boys and bubble-o,
>> Under the broom.

Thomas Hardy and the Piddle Valley

Dorset's greatest literary figure is, of course, Thomas Hardy. He took much of the West Country to make up the Wessex of his novels and poems, endowing real places with names of his own invention so that he could adjust their features to suit his needs unrestricted by real-life geography. Because of this, many of his admirers find added interest in tracing the origins of such places as Casterbridge, Budmouth and Weatherbury.

His name for the Piddle Valley villages was Longpuddle. Sometimes this is divided into Upper and Lower Longpuddle, and it is tempting to equate these with Piddletrenthide and Piddlehinton respectively. But in practice it is not as neat as this since he tended to amalgamate the two villages into one if it suited him to do so.

The work in which Longpuddle figures most prominently is *A Few Crusted Characters*, a collection of short sketches which deserves to be better known than it is, as it embraces the whole Hardy range from naturalistic to fanciful, serious to knockabout farce. The thread on which the sketches hang is a journey home from 'a well-known market town' by an assortment of villagers in the van belonging to 'Burthen, Carrier to Longpuddle'. Among the company is an apparent stranger who turns out to be a returning native, and the others bring him up to date by telling him stories of what his neighbours have been up to during his absence.

Some of the places mentioned need no detective work to identify them. The well-known market town, with its White Hart Inn and 'clock in the turret at the top of the street', is of course Dorchester, for both landmarks are still there. And the second bridge out of the town, 'behind which, as every native remembers, the road takes a turn, and travellers by this highway disappear finally from the view of the gazing burghers,' is Gray's Bridge, that same bridge from which the ruined and bitter Michael Henchard in *The Mayor of Casterbridge* wandered and would have ended his miserable life had he not been dismayed to see what he thought was an effigy of himself floating down the stream. There is mention in more than one story of the 'corner where we turn round to drop down the hill to Lower Longpuddle', and this steeply dipping approach to Piddlehinton is still there, in spite of road improvements. Other places require a little detective work. For instance, in *A Few Crusted Characters* Hardy mentions 'the church', but there are two to choose from and so which one had he in mind? The subject of the story in question is a favourite of Hardy's – the 'quire' of strings and woodwind that accompanied church services before organs became popular. They played in a gallery at the west end of the church 'and 'twas so mortal cold that year that they could hardly sit in the gallery'; as Piddletrenthide had such a gallery at the time of these stories and Piddlehinton had not, it has to be Piddletrenthide. The gallery has since gone, but today's congregation will tell you that the cold has not! Piddletrenthide Manor House is also mentioned and 'Longpuddle Spring', which we know as Morning Well, the place where seven springs bubble out of the ground behind the church.

A few of Hardy's poems owe their being to the Piddle Valley. 'A Sunday Morning Tragedy' tells of a girl from the Pydel Vale who loved not wisely but too well and of the tragic outcome of her mother's interference in the affair. 'The Sexton of Longpuddle' shows the poet in mordant vein as the sexton contemplates the graves in the churchyard and ghoulishly reflects that he at least will never lack for work. 'We Field-Women' takes place in the weather-swept world of 'Flintcomb-Ash', where rain soaks the women as they work at trimming swedes or snow drives them under cover to the Great Barn to draw reeds.

And this brings us to *Tess of the d'Urbervilles*, perhaps Hardy's best-known novel. Flintcomb-Ash, the 'starve-acre place' where Tess toiled in the swede fields after she had been deserted by Angel Clare, is certainly situated on the uplands above the northern end of the Piddle but its actual whereabouts is still the subject of debate. The isolated farm of Dole's Ash, a mile to the east of Piddletrenthide, is an obvious contender by virtue of its name, but it probably lies too far to the south to fit the walk that Tess took from there to Beaminster. It must, all the same, have grieved Hardy not to use the name of Dole's Ash as it expresses so perfectly Tess's forlorn circumstances; but that was not his custom, although he did use the 'Ash' part to symbolize the burnt-out relics of Tess's hopes of happiness. Church Hill and Barcombe Down, both north-east of Alton St Pancras, are more likely candidates for the doubtful honour of providing the miserable setting for Hardy's most famous heroine. They are close to the bridle path which runs due west towards Beaminster and, what is more, for the first version of his novel Hardy chose the name 'Alton Ash', only changing it later to the harder-sounding Flintcomb.

Hardy must have known the Piddle Valley well, for his sister Mary, with whom he had a very close relationship described by Robert Gittings as something like that between Wordsworth and his sister Dorothy, became the school mistress at Piddlehinton in 1870 and he must often have accompanied her on her daily journey to the village. At this time he had returned, as she had, to the family home at Higher Bockhampton. He spent much time with his mother's relatives in Puddletown and from there to the Piddle Valley is no distance, particularly if one goes by way

of Waterston Manor, used by Hardy as Bathsheba Everdene's farm house in *Far from the Madding Crowd*.

Hardy had a further connection with the Valley. In early life he was apprenticed to a Dorchester architect, John Hicks, and Hicks had a brother, James, who was vicar of All Saints, Piddletrenthide, for forty-three years. Parson Hicks concerned himself continually with the restoration and renovation of his church and called on his brother to act as architect for these improvements. It is therefore quite probable that John Hicks's young apprentice accompanied his master to the church many times in the course of his duties. During these visits no doubt he noticed the two Dumberfield headstones that stand slightly askew in the churchyard, both dated 1616 – for from the name of this family he devised the surname of the d'Urbervilles.

FRANCES MALLETT

MAX GATE

In the summer of 1885 Thomas Hardy moved to Max Gate, outside Dorchester, a house which he designed himself and which was to be his home for over forty years. One of Piddletrenthide's oldest inhabitants, Mr Bob Jesty, remembers the time when, as a young boy, he was sent with a school friend to take tea with the famous writer each week. His recollections of those regular meetings, of little interest to a small boy unable to appreciate the special greatness of the ageing genius, have prompted these lines from an admiring acquaintance:

> So we went to tea. Little he was and pale,
> Fretful and fidgety, sunk in his favourite chair,
> With the sun shut out and an old man's smell in the air.
> Each week we went, and the cakes were always stale.

'Wipe your feet and hang your coat on the nail,
Sit with your hands in your lap and drink your tea.
One day you'll be proud to say: "He spoke with me,"'
Well, he mumbled a bit and the cakes were always stale.

Two little boys, who looked in vain for a tale
Of hero and knight as they sat and swung their feet.
'At least there'll be scones and jam and a cake to eat,
A curranty cake.' But the cake was always stale.

How could we know, with the air like an old man's breath,
How could we know there was greatness there in the room,
With the carpet faded and frayed, and a dusty bloom
On the mantel shelf . . . and the cakes as dry as death?

I'm an old man now and my memory starts to fail.
Did I really touch that hand and see that face?
Was genius really alive in that homely place?
And the cakes . . . ? Well, at least I know they were always stale!

M.P.

159